ONLINE RESOURCES FOR CAREGIVERS OF THE ELDERLY

Charles C. Sharpe

McFarland & Company, Inc., Publishers
Jefferson, North Carolina, and London

LIBRARY OF CONGRESS CATALOGUING-IN-PUBLICATION DATA

Sharpe, Charles C., 1935–
Online resources for caregivers of the elderly /
Charles C. Sharpe.
p.   cm.
Includes bibliographical references and index.

ISBN 978-0-7864-5941-4
softcover : 50# alkaline paper

1. Caregivers— Services for — United States—
Computer network resources.
2. Older people — Care — United States—
Computer network resources.   I. Title.
RA645.35.S49   2010   362'.04250285 — dc22   2010016071

British Library cataloguing data are available

Cover image ©2010 Shutterstock

Manufactured in the United States of America

*McFarland & Company, Inc., Publishers
Box 611, Jefferson, North Carolina 28640
www.mcfarlandpub.com*

Contents

Preface

"All the world's a stage, ...
And one man in his time plays many parts,
His acts being seven ages. At first the infant,
Mewling and puking in the nurse's arms,
... Last scene of all,
That ends this strange eventful history,
Is second childishness and mere oblivion;
Sans teeth, sans eyes, sans taste, sans everything."
— Shakespeare, *As You Like It*, Act II, Scene VII

Were he alive today, the Bard might recognize an eighth stage, one which philosophers and poets through the centuries have observed: that parents and children often reverse roles as the parents grow older and, so often, enter into that "second childishness." At these times, the child — son or daughter — becomes, metaphorically, the parent of his or her frail, elderly, helpless parent or parents. Perhaps "parental figure" would be a more accurate description of the role reversal.

It can be an abrupt or gradual transition; easy or difficult. There may be willingness and acceptance on both sides; there may be stubborn resistance or inevitable resignation. There may be rivalries and recriminations. It will never be easy. Unfortunately for all concerned, most of us have not been taught how to deal with it and are not prepared to cope with this role reversal when and if it should occur.

The baby boomers are turning 65, and this has been described as the "graying of America" or the "silver tsunami." As a nation, we are not prepared to provide proper support for the more than 48 million men and women who are now caring for older family members and friends. Of these, there are at least 43.5 million who provide unpaid care to an adult family member or friend who is age 50 or older. The average age of today's caregiver is 50; the average age of today's

1

care recipient is 77. As the baby boom generation ages over the next 25 years, the proportions of individuals needing care will increase. The numbers of younger persons available to provide care will decrease. This suggests that in the future, caregivers will be older, on average, than today's caregivers, and could have greater infirmity of their own. The old and infirm may be caregivers of the very old and very infirm.

When we think about the future, few, if any, of us ever imagine that it could include the role of caring for an elderly parent, relative, or friend — a role you may have or might reluctantly assume. You may be a spouse, child, neighbor, close friend, or a distant relative of an elderly person in need of care. You could even be the elderly child of an elderly parent caring for you. Regardless of your age, as a caregiver you must be prepared to make concessions and sacrifices. You will likely have personal plans and goals that must be interrupted, drastically modified, or abandoned because of your responsibilities.

Caregiving may be one of the most important roles you will undertake in your lifetime. Typically it is not an easy experience, nor is it one for which most of us are prepared. Like most people, you may have questions about how to cope with your care receiver's illnesses or disability. If you have a job and are juggling several responsibilities, or if your family member or friend needs a great deal of assistance, you yourself may need help. Whether you are expecting to become a caregiver or have been thrust into the role, it is essential that you know where you can get information and such help. That is the purpose of this guide.

Caregivers are a diverse group whose caregiving experiences range from those that are minimally involved in providing care, and who enjoy a relatively easy experience managing their care recipient's needs. These suffer little negative impact on their own emotional, physical, or financial lives. On the other hand, a smaller proportion of caregivers carry a heavy burden which inevitably takes a toll on them by increasing their vulnerability to physical strain, emotional stress, and financial hardships ... they burn out. This book will provide access to the resources that may enhance your caregiving efforts, and the life of those for whom you care, and alleviate the conflicts and stress caused by the demands of caregiving.

You may find caregiving to be highly satisfying and personally rewarding or a completely frustrating function that can create areas of conflict and high levels of stress in your life and in the lives of all others involved — situations for which you may not be adequately prepared.

It is hoped that this book will facilitate such preparation and will help to:

- Educate you about where you can get help — both before and when you need it.

- Guide you in exploring a variety of options.
- Assist you in planning — to be prepared before the inevitable crises.
- Enhance communication with all parties and stifle conflicts.
- Assess your personal responsibilities and resources — including coping skills.
- Enable you to deal with your feelings in what may be a painful transition.
- Help prevent burnout — to care for yourself so that you can care for a loved one.

This book is intended as a guide that offers a range of suggestions to make caregiving easier and more successful, whether you are a caregiver or the person who ensures that your loved one receives the best possible care from others. The content was derived entirely from the wealth of information which can be readily accessed on the World Wide Web. It organizes the information to address particular aspects of caregiving. The more than 250 web sites listed offer a range of information that caregivers can use. Hyperlinks on each site present innumerable other sources.

Caregiving demands time, effort, and devotion. You will be challenged physically, intellectually, and emotionally. Even when those being cared for are not able to improve, your efforts are enhancing the life of someone you care so much about, someone you love; who, in Shakespeare's seventh stage, "sans everything," has now, perhaps, become your child and, in pathetic reversion, also as "At first the infant."

Caregivers

A caregiver is any individual who provides various types of assistance, to varying degrees, to any person who is ill or disabled — chronically or temporarily — or simply in need of help for any reason.

The word "caregiver" typically brings to mind an image of a professional such as a nurse, nursing assistant, home health aide, or anyone employed in the capacity. These are considered "formal" caregivers, and usually are trained, licensed, or certified. However, research has shown that most individuals acting in the role are members of the family — spouse, child, relative — or a friend of the care recipient who volunteer their services. These latter are referred to as "informal caregivers." Often they are, themselves, older. And it is they who are the primary source of care for the largest majority of the reliant older adults who live in the community — our focus here. This book has been prepared as an invaluable resource to those functioning in either role.

What do caregivers do? The elderly person may be chronically ill, physically disabled, mentally incapacitated, all of these, or non of these. Depending on their specific needs, caregiving can involve a variety activities of daily living. These might include:

- medications
- toileting
- bathing
- dressing
- meal preparation
- eating
- managing affairs
- cleaning
- shopping
- social

Other tasks or duties might involve those related to the elderly person's specific illness or disability. These might include a regimen or turning, and exercising — such as range of motion.

In November 2009, in the report *Caregiving in the U.S. 2009*, published by AARP in collaboration with the National Alliance for Caregiving (NAC), researchers found that:

1. In the past 12 months, an estimated 65.7 million people in the U.S. have served as unpaid family caregivers to an adult or child. About 28.5 of the respondents surveyed (1,480 chosen at random) reported being caregivers. The percentage of people who are caregivers does not appear to have changed significantly since 2004.

2. More than three in ten (31.2 percent) of all U.S. households report that at least one person has served as an unpaid family caregiver within the last twelve months, leading to an estimate of 36.5 million households with a caregiver present. Statistically nearly one in every three homes in every neighborhood, in every community, across the nation includes a caregiver (AARP, NAC, *Caregiving in the U.S. 2009*, p. 4).

   Family members not social service agencies, nursing homes, or government programs, are the mainstay underpinning long term care for older and disabled persons in the United States. One person is usually the primary caregiver, although there may be other family and friends that help.

3. The degree of caregiver involvement has remained fairly constant for more than a decade, bearing witness to the remarkable resilience of the American family in taking care of its older persons. This is despite increased geographic separation, greater numbers of women in the workforce, and other changes in family life.

In report derived from the above study, *A Focused Look at Those Caring for Someone Age 50 or Older*, the authors stated:

We estimate there are at least 43.5 million caregivers age 18 and over, equivalent to 19 percent of adults, who provide unpaid care to an adult family member or friend who is age 50 years or older." At the broadest level there caregivers are:
- female (67 percent), and 50 years of age, on average
- white (76 percent)
- married (59 percent)
- caring for one person (70 percent)
- assisting a relative (89 percent)

- providing care for an average of four to five years
- providing 19 hours of care in an average week
- employed while caregiving (55 percent) (AARP, NAC, *A Focused Look at Those Caring for Someone Age 50 or Older*, 2009, p. 14).

The main reasons this population needs care are:

- depredations of old age (12 percent)
- Alzheimer's disease (10 percent)
- mental/emotional illness (7 percent)
- cancer (7 percent)
- heart disease (5 percent)
- stroke (5 percent).

Note: Because of the increasing incidence of Alzheimer's Disease (AD) in the population, the Web has a large number of sites (7,000,000 +) dealing with the topic and resources for caregivers. A select few have been included in this book. For a discussion of caregiving for a person with AD, the reader is referred to Appendix D, *Caregiver Guide — Tips for Caregivers of People with Alzheimer's Disease.*

THE SANDWICH GENERATION

One aspect of caregiving that is currently receiving a great deal of attention is the so-called "sandwich generation," defined as the generation of middle-aged individuals who are pressured to support both aging parents and growing children. They are caught between obligations to care for their parents— who may be ill, unable to perform various tasks, or in need of financial support — and those toward their children, who may still require financial, physical, and emotional support. These obligations demand considerable time and money. With the added burdens of employment and personal issues, as well as the need to contribute to their own retirement, the individuals of the sandwich generation are under significant stress.

According to the Pew Research Center, just over one of every eight Americans aged forty to sixty is both raising a child and caring for a parent. Between seven to ten million adults are caring for their aging parents from a long distance. U.S. Census Bureau statistics indicate that the number of older Americans aged sixty or older will double by the year 2030, to over seventy million. The anticipated increases in longevity predicted in U.S. society in the coming decades will increase the likelihood that middle-aged individuals will inevitably assume the role of caregiver for their parents when they, themselves, have grown old. (Pew Research Center, 2005).

On her website The Sandwich Generation (www.thesandwichgeneration. com), Carol Abaya, a leading expert in this area, categorizes the different scenarios involved in being a part of the sandwich generation. Her menu metaphor:

- Traditional: those sandwiched between aging parents who need care and/or help and their own children.
- Club Sandwich: those in their 50s or 60s sandwiched between aging parents, adult children and grandchildren, or those in their 30s and 40s, with young children, aging parents and grandparents.
- Open Faced: anyone else involved in elder care.

In his first State of the Union Address on January 27, 2010, President Obama outlined a series of economic initiatives aimed at helping struggling middle class/middle income families—families that are sometimes called "the missing middle" because government child-care and elder-care policies offer them so little help. These initiatives included a key theme — aid for families taking care of elderly relatives.

This is a two-pronged approach. First, the Obama plan would increase the child and dependent-care tax credit for middle-income Americans. Though many people focus on this as a child-care credit, it also can be claimed by people taking care of older parents who live with them, and whom they can claim as dependents. The second piece of the caregivers package cheered many organizations that work directly with caregivers. It would add $102 million in direct funding to state and local aging offices so they could provide more guidance, meals, transportation, and other services. This could increase the budgets of these programs by a third.

A White House Fact Sheet, released on January 25, 2010, stated: "At the same time, middle class families in the 'sandwich generation'—struggling to care for both their children and their parents—will also benefit from new initiatives to support elder care for seniors, and respite for their caregivers." The Fact Sheet — "Helping Middle Class Families Care for Aging Relatives" affirms that:

An estimated 38 million Americans provide unpaid care to an aging relative, including approximately 23 million caregivers with jobs and 12 million who are also caring for their own children. The $102.5 million Caregiver Initiative will ease the burden on families with elder care responsibilities and allow seniors to live in the community for as long as possible. The Initiative adds $52.5 million in funding to Department of Health and Human Services caregiver support programs that provide temporary respite care, counseling, training, and referrals to critical services.

The extra funding will allow nearly 200,000 additional caregivers to be served and 3 million more hours of respite care to be provided. It also adds $50 million to programs that provide transportation help, adult day care, and in-home services, such as aides to help seniors bathe and cook, help which eases the burden for family members and helps seniors stay in their homes.

In a 2007 study, AARP estimated the economic value of 34 million family and informal caregivers to be approximately $375 billion, up from an estimated $350 billion in 2006. This amount exceeded total Medicaid long-term care spending in all states. The costs of caregiving to the caregivers themselves are incalculable. Such costs cannot be measured by a simple tabulation of hours. They include direct out-of-pocket expenses incurred which can be defined, but also the immeasurable toll on caregivers' physical and psychological well being (AARP, 2008).

SUMMARY

Gail Hunt, president and CEO of the National Alliance for Caregiving has said: "More and more people who are 65-plus are providing care to both children and adults.... The shift to an older population of caregivers points to a real need for assistance for these individuals from family, friends, employers and social service programs. With more support for caregiving, older and disabled people would be able to do what is so important to them, to remain in their own homes with those they love" (Hunt, 2009).

REFERENCES

AARP, "Valuing the Invaluable: The Economic Value of Family Caregiving." http://www.aarp.org/research/housing-mobility/caregiving/i13_caregiving.html, December 29, 2008.

AARP, National Alliance for Caregiving, *A Focused Look at Those Caring for Someone Age 50 or Older*. http://assets.aarp.org/rgcenter/il/caregiving_09_es50.pdf, November 2009.

AARP, National Alliance for Caregiving. *Caregiving in the U.S. 2009*. http://www.aarp.org/research/surveys/care/ltc/hc/articles/caregiving_09.html, November 2009.

Hunt, Gail. "Nearly a Third of All US Adults Are Now Family Caregivers—65.7 Million." *The Caregiver's Home Companion*. http://caregivershome.com/news/article.cfm?UID=2341, December 15, 2009.

Pew Research Center. "Baby Boomers: From the Age of Aquarius to the Age of Responsibility." http://pewsocialtrends.org/pubs/306/baby-boomers-from-the-age-of-aquarius-to-the-age-of-responsibility, December 8, 2005.

Caregiver Stress

Caring for an older adult can be immensely rewarding and fulfilling, but the experience can also place great physical, emotional, and financial demands on the caregiver whose needs are likely to become secondary to those of the aged person in need of care. Failing to address those needs can lead to physical and psychological problems including depression and stress.

Caregiver stress is, very simply, the emotional strain of caregiving. Stress is often described as the body's "fight or flight" response to danger. When the body goes on "high alert" to protect itself, essential functions, like respiration and heart rate, speed up, while less immediate functions, such as the immune system, slow down. Although the stress response is a healthy reaction, the body needs to repair itself once danger is removed. For caregivers, whose stress often results from fatigue and conflicts that never go away, their bodies never get a chance to heal. If the immune system isn't functioning fully, the caregiver is at greater risk for infections and disease. Some experts believe that stress causes hypertension, coronary disease, or even premature death. Such stress is increasingly being referred to in the medical community as "caregiver syndrome."

Caring for another person takes a great deal of time and effort and many caregivers must juggle that time and effort with full-time jobs and/or parenting. In the process, they often put their own needs aside. Unfortunately, a significant number of family caregivers describe their own health as "fair to poor." They often report that it is difficult to look after their own health in terms of exercise, nutrition, and physician visits when necessary. As a consequence, caregivers frequently experience feelings of anger, anxiety, isolation, sadness, and varying degrees of depression.

Studies have shown that:

- Caregivers are more likely to suffer from depression than their peers. The more hours spent on caregiving, the greater the risk of anxiety and depression.

- Those who care for their spouses are more prone to caregiving-related stress than those who care for other family members.
- Female caregivers are particularly prone to feeling stress and overwhelmed; and typically have more emotional and physical health problems, employment-related problems, and financial strain than male caregivers.
- Those who care for people with Alzheimer's disease or other kinds of dementia are likely to suffer from depression and stress, and are particularly vulnerable to burnout.
- Caregivers are also more likely to have health problems than non-caregivers.
- When it comes to their health, caregivers are less likely than their peers of the same age to engage in health-promoting behaviors and take steps that are important for chronic disease prevention and control.

Some barriers for family caregivers, which often prevent their participation in health promotion and disease prevention activities, include:

- the guilt that caregivers may feel by taking time out to care for themselves
- competing demands on caregivers' time
- ability to provide, and availability of, respite care
- availability and access to health promotion services, education, and information

DO ALL CAREGIVERS EXPERIENCE STRESS?

Some degree stress in a caregiving role is a normal physiological response. Historically it was believed that the more care provided, the greater degree of stress. Now we know that all caregivers are not created equal. Some, who provide high levels of care, experience no stress, while others who provide relatively little care experience high levels. Many experts believe that these differences can be explained by subjective factors such as how caregivers feel about providing care, their current and past relationships to those they care for, and their personal coping abilities. Some caregivers find certain behaviors by care receivers to be particularly stressful, including aggression, combativeness, wandering, and incontinence. Others report that they experience stress because they don't get enough rest, privacy, support, or time for themselves

Providing care for someone you love who is no longer able to take care of him- or herself produces a wide range of emotions. It is natural to feel sadness and grief for your loved one's losses and for the loss of your own previous life — your freedom. If you have any of the following emotions or experiences—continually, pervasively—caregiving may be causing too much stress:

- helpless
- change in appetite
- weight gain or loss
- fatigue
- loneliness
- isolation
- loss of interest
- physical problems
- anger
- sadness
- resentment
- guilt
- impatience
- shame
- anxiety
- irritation
- frustration
- overwhelmed
- self pity — the "martyr" role

Some of these emotions or experiences may shock you or seem "bad." These feelings are not self-centered or wicked. It is a normal response to the extreme changes that providing care can bring to your life.

It is important to note that caring for another person can also create positive emotional change. Aside from feeling stress, many caregivers say their role has had many positive effects on their lives. For example, caregivers report that caregiving has given them a sense of purpose. They say that their role makes them feel useful, capable, and that they are making a difference in the life of a loved one.

By developing effective coping strategies, you may be able to avoid reaching the point of exhaustion and burnout. Do not let it go that far!

As a caregiver, you invest a great deal of your time and energy to meet someone else's needs, and often ignore your own. When difficult emotions surface, remember that you have your own needs. Let your feelings prompt you to do something for yourself. Your first priority is *take care of yourself!* Taking care of oneself is essential if your best care is to be provided to another person. Caregivers must learn how to balance their own needs with the needs of someone who needs care. In the process, they will become better caregivers.

The causes of stress vary with the responsibilities and the caregiver. What creates stress for you may not create stress for someone else. Once you know the sources of stress, you must determine which ones you can do something about and which are beyond your control. Successful coping involves accepting what you can and cannot change.

COPING STRATEGIES

Consider these strategies in dealing with stress:

- Get help when needed. Professionals are available and a third party analyzing the situation can be a reliable ally. The Internet is another resource for finding help nationally and in your community. The many resources listed in this book will prove invaluable in getting such help.
- Educate yourself about the disease or medical condition you are dealing with. Whether you care for someone with heart disease, stroke, or dementia, or whether care takes place in your own home or at a distance, many of the daily challenges are similar.
- Find an eldercare specialist, a trained expert, who can help you find the services and support you need. Consult with other experts as needed. Other than health care, you may need additional professional help. For instance:
  1. You may need legal authority to make healthcare and financial decisions on behalf of the individual you are caring for.
  2. A certified financial planner may help you prepare for the possibility of expensive care in an assisted-living facility or other chronic-care facility.
  3. Getting experts involved as soon as possible may save you a lot of worry later.
  4. If you are too busy to attend to these matters, make sure someone who is competent to do so acts in your behalf to handle them.

- Identify all of the community resources in your area that may be available. Find these resources early. You may not need them now, but you will have them when you need them. Unfortunately, many caregivers delay looking for help until they are exhausted.

- Tap your social networks. Other family members and friends can play key roles in helping you to share in the care. Don't be afraid to ask for help; don't do it all yourself. Use your family, friends, or neighbors for support. Family may help share caregiving tasks. Friends and neighbors may help with other chores. Ask for and accept help — even that you do not ask for.

- Stay in touch with friends and family. Social activities can help you feel connected and may reduce stress.

- Find a confidante such as a good friend or counselor to share your own emotional burden and learn ways to cope effectively. Having someone to talk with about your frustrations can be helpful. A person who needs care can sometimes be angry or depressed about being dependent, and you make an easy target for the venting of negative emotions. It is difficult to be compassionate if the person you care for is upset with you. It is seldom helpful to confront him or her about the ill effects their disability is having on you.

- Set priorities and realistic goals — make lists and establish a daily routine. Keeping a calendar of activities helps to identify priorities. Accustomed to doing things in a hurry,? you may be surprised to find out how little you can accomplish when you are responsible for another person. Be patient. Set small, realistic, goals for yourself each day or week and build upon your successes instead of thinking about your failings. Learn to appreciate that you are making progress in ensuring that both you and the person in your care are getting the best possible care. Celebrate your achievements.

- According to your personal convictions, explore religious beliefs and spiritual values. Caring for someone with a chronic illness often evokes questions about faith, hope, God and the meaning of life. Individual and group prayer, rituals, meditation, inspirational reading, and spiritual direction may provide help.

- Talk about your feelings. Reach out to others (friends, family, clergy) — this will help reduce feelings of isolation.

- Join a support group for caregivers in your situation. Support groups provide caregivers with the opportunity to share with other caregivers and learn from one another. Many support groups can be found in the community or on the Internet.

- Try to get enough sleep and rest.
- Eat healthy foods and do not skip meals. Ask your physician about taking a multivitamin.
- See your physician for a checkup — at least yearly. Tell him or her that you are a caregiver. Discuss any symptoms of stress you may be having.
- *Make time for you.* Take some time each day for relaxation and exercise — to do something for *yourself* — otherwise you risk losing yourself to the exclusive needs of another person. Diversions are necessary in order to be renewed. Take care of yourself in ways that are meaningful to you. Do whatever it takes to nurture yourself. Do things that are important to you.
- Maintain your sense of humor. Taking a lighthearted view can alter the meaning of a situation that might otherwise appear overwhelmingly depressing.
- Give yourself credit not guilt.
- Take one day at a time.

Remember you are not alone. You are among the nearly 44 million Americans who care for older parents, in-laws, grandparents, and other older loved ones.

COMMUNITY RESOURCES

Check the local Area Agency on Aging, which administers state and federal funds to help older chronically ill persons and their family caregivers. To find your local agency, check the yellow pages or contact the Eldercare Locator — www.eldercare.gov. Contact other local agencies which may help you get a well-deserved break by providing in-home services—free or at a nominal cost.

Family Issues—
Stresses and Conflicts

As most families know, "conflict happens." Families involved with making decisions about the care of an adult (or a minor) family member know how stressful this endeavor can be and the conflicts that it can engender—for the care provider, recipient, and all family members involved. Conflict is not always a bad thing. However, those unprepared for conflict are, typically, not able to resolve it in a positive way.

This chapter provides an overview of areas of potential conflict that might arise in family caregiving and includes strategies for resolving such issues when they occur.

AREAS OF POTENTIAL CONFLICT

The easiest way to avoid caregiving conflict is for a care receiver, whenever possible, to plan in advance. However, not everyone is able to make their wishes known or to make such preparations. Caregiving conflict can arise around a wide range of issues, including, but not limited to:

Living arrangements: If not remaining in their own home
- With whom?
- Where?
- When?
- How long?
- Who decides?
- Degree of independence?

Household care and maintenance: If remaining in their own home
- What options are available for ongoing services?
- What services are needed and how frequently?

Healthcare decisions
- Who should/will provide care?
- What care is needed?
- Who should make medical decisions?

Financial decisions
- How should money be spent?
- How should investments be handled?
- How will concerns over "unwise spending," etc. be handled?

Communication Issues
- What information is needed or missing?
- Who has legal authority to access information?
- How will information be shared with those who need it?
- How should the family deal with sibling rivalries, new spouse or companion, death of a spouse/caregiver, other changes in relationships?

Decision-making
- Who should have authority to make decisions?
- What input (if any) should others have?
- How can decision makers obtain input from the care receiver?

Safety/risk taking/autonomy
- What safety issues are identified?
- Is the level of risk understood and acceptable?
- Should autonomy be limited?

Respite care and support for caregivers
- What services are needed to support the caregivers?
- What services are available locally?
- What resources are available or can be used to pay for needed services?

Needs of other family members/caregivers
- Are there competing needs of other care receivers such as dependent children or grandchildren?

RESOLVING CONFLICT

Sometimes it is hard to see another person's point of view, particularly in family situations where strong emotions are at play. The following tips can help address conflict in a positive way and prevent it from escalating:

Plan a time to talk things over and set an agenda
- Focus the agenda on the issues that are causing conflict.
- Keep it focused. Don't discuss too much in one meeting.
- Set additional meetings for other issues if necessary.

Practice good communication skills
- Clearly say what is important to you and why you feel that way. Use "I" statements to explain how you feel and why.
- Speak for yourself and let others raise issues of importance to them.
- Separate the people from the problem. Look at the problem objectively and try to avoid assigning blame.
- Focus on interests (WHY someone feels, believes or wants a certain thing) rather than positions (WHAT someone feels, believes or wants).
- Focus on how things might work in the future. Don't dwell on past problems.
- Try to respond to one another in a way that is not defensive and hostile. (This can be difficult!)

Practice "active listening" techniques
- Let everyone speak without interruption.
- Listen to what they are saying is important to them.
- Repeat what you thought was said to be sure you understand how others are feeling.
- Ask family members to pretend they are another family member who has the opposite view. Then ask them what their interests are and why they feel as they do.

Involve the care recipient

- Try to involve and respect the wishes of the care receiver in caregiving conflicts whenever possible. So often, it will not be.
- If the care receiver cannot tell you what they want or is making unsafe choices, look to that person's life long values and beliefs for guidance rather than deciding what you think would be best.

Gather needed information

- Is more information, are more resources needed to make a decision?
- Figure out where and how to get the information.
- Who will get it and how will it be shared?
- Schedule an additional meeting if necessary, after everyone has reviewed the new information.

ENGAGE A MEDIATOR

When families are unable to resolve caregiving problems on their own, it may be useful to involve a trained, neutral third party such as a mediator. Such a professional can provide a confidential, private setting in which everyone's concerns can be heard and addressed. They use a process that is fair and unbiased, and allow the participants to make decisions about the outcome.

Respite Care — Care for the Caregiver

Millions of Americans provide unpaid assistance each year to elderly family, friends, and neighbors to help them remain in their own homes and communities for as long as possible. At times these caregivers need time off to relax or take care of other responsibilities. This is where respite care can be helpful. It provides the family caregivers with the break they need, and also ensures that their elderly loved one is still receiving the attention that he or she needs.

All respite care is not the same. It can vary in time from part of a day to several weeks. The concept encompasses a wide variety of services including traditional home-based care, as well as adult day care, skilled nursing, home health, and short term institutional care. More specifically such care may take any one of the following forms:

- Adult Day Care:
    These programs are designed to provide care and companionship for frail and disabled persons who need assistance or supervision. They offer relief to family members or caregivers and allows them the freedom to go to work, attend to personal business, or just relax while knowing their relative is well cared for and safe.

- Informal and Volunteer Respite Care:
    This is as simple as it sounds. It is accepting help from other family members, friends, neighbors, or other volunteers who offer to stay with the elderly individual while you go to the store or run other errands. Sometimes an area agency on aging will run a "Friendly Visitor Program" in which volunteers provide basic respite care. Many communities have formed either "Interfaith Caregiver" or "Faith in Action" programs where volunteers from faith-based groups are matched with caregivers to provide them with some relief.

- In-home respite care:

    Generally speaking, in-home respite care involves the following four types of services:

    1. Companion services to help the family caregiver to supervise, entertain, or just visit with the senior when he or she is lonely and wants company.
    2. Homemaker services to assist with housekeeping chores, preparing meals, or shopping.
    3. Personal care services to help the aged individual bathe, dress, go to the bathroom, and/or exercise.
    4. Skilled care services to assist the family caregiver in tending to the senior's medical needs, such as administering medications, assisting in treatments, etc.

The cost of respite care varies with the type of agency and the services needed, but federal and/or state programs may help to pay for it. Long-term care insurance policies may cover some of the cost of respite. Your local area agency on aging will have more information on whether financial assistance is available, depending on your situation and where you live.

The enactment of the Older Americans Act Amendments of 2000 (Public Law 106-501) established The National Family Caregiver Support Program (NFCSP). Funds have been allocated to states to work in partnership with area agencies on aging and local and community service providers to put into place multi-faceted systems of support for family caregivers. A specific component of these systems is respite. That could include, for example, respite care provided in a home, an adult day-care program or over a weekend in a nursing home or an assisted living facility. (For more information on the NFCSP see the entry in Resources.)

HOW TO ENSURE THAT RESPITE CARE IS QUALITY CARE

When evaluating a respite care program, family members should check to see if it is licensed by the state in which they live (where required), and if the caregivers have the necessary qualifications. They can ask respite care providers or program managers the following questions to assess their credentials:

- Are families limited to a certain number of hours for services needed?
- Can the provider take care of more than one person at a time?

- Can family members meet and interview the people who will be providing the respite care?
- Does the program provide transportation for the caregiver/senior?
- Does the program keep an active file on the senior's medical condition and other needs? Will they prepare a written care plan?
- How are the caregivers screened for their jobs?
- How are the caregivers trained? Do they receive extra training, where appropriate, to meet specific family needs?
- How are the caregivers supervised and evaluated? By whom?
- How much does the respite care cost? What is included in the fee?
- How far ahead of time do family members have to call to arrange services?
- How do the caregivers handle emergencies? What instructions do they receive to prepare them for unexpected situations?
- How is the program evaluated? Are family members contacted for their feedback?

HIRING AN IN-HOME AIDE

When interviewing an in-home respite care aide, you may want to ask these questions:

- Are you insured? bonded?
- Do you have any references? Who are they?
- Do you have any special skills that might help you with this job?
- Have you ever worked with someone in the same medical condition as my loved one?
- How would you handle the following situation? (Cite hypothetical examples of challenges you have encountered as a family caregiver.)
- What is your background and training?
- What are your past experiences in providing respite care?
- When are you available? Do you have a back-up/assistant if you are unable to come when expected?

- Whom can I talk to at your agency if I am concerned about something? Are they always available?
- Why are you interested in this job?
- Why did you leave your last job?

MORE ABOUT RESPITE SERVICES

The following organizations provide useful information to caregivers on a variety of topics including respite. The reader is referred to the entry for each for additional information.

- The Alzheimer's Association provides education and support for people diagnosed with the condition, their families, and caregivers. To find a local chapter closest to you or to order a copy of the association's respite care guide visit their website at www.alz.org or call 800-272-3900.

- The Family Caregiver Alliance (FCA) runs a resource center and publishes fact sheets and a newsletter with tips for family caregivers. The organization can be reached by calling 1-415-434-3388 or visiting its website at: http://www.caregiver.org.

- The National Alliance for Caregiving (NAC) is a joint venture of several private and governmental agencies. The alliance web site provides useful information and links for caregivers. You can contact this resource by visiting its website at: http://www.caregiving.org.

- National Adult Day Services Association. Information concerning adult day services can be obtained from the Association at (703) 610-9005 or by visiting their website at: http://www.nadsa.org.

HOSPICE CARE

To find out more about hospice programs where you live, you can contact your local aging information and assistance provider or area agency on aging (AAA). The Eldercare Locator, a public service of the Administration on Aging (www.eldercare.gov) can help connect you to these agencies.

FURTHER READING

You are referred to *Care for the Family Caregiver — A Place to Start.* This 46 page brochure from the National Alliance for Caregiving (NAC) can be downloaded at: http://www.caregiving.org/pubs/brochures/CFC.pdf.

Evaluating Health
Care Information
on the Internet

Millions of consumers obtain health information from magazines, TV, or the myriad of health-related websites on the Internet. Regarding the latter, some of the information is reliable and current; some of it is not. Some is downright dangerous. How can you tell the good from the bad? Choosing which website to trust can be a challenge.

As a rule, those websites sponsored by federal government agencies are good sources of authoritative health information. You can reach all federal websites by visiting www.usa.gov. A premier site is that of the National Library of Medicine (NLM) (http://www.nlm.nih.gov/). Another is the NLM's MedlinePlus site (www.medlineplus.gov) for dependable information on more than 700 health-related topics. An excellent source of reliable information is the National Institutes of Health (NIH) (www.nih.gov). Start here to find information on almost every health topic. You can also visit NIHSeniorHealth (www.nihseniorhealth. gov)—a website with health information designed specifically for older people. It is a senior-friendly website from the National Institute on Aging and the National Library of Medicine.

The NLM offers "Evaluating Internet Health Information: A Tutorial." This tutorial teaches you how to evaluate the health information that you find on the Web. It is about 16 minutes long. You need a Flash plug-in, version 6 or above, to view it. If you do not have the Flash plug-in, you will be prompted to obtain a free download of the software before you start. The tutorial runs automatically, but you can also use the navigation bar at the bottom of the screen to go forward, backward, pause, or start over. The tutorial can be found at: http://www. nlm.nih.gov/medlineplus/webeval/webeval.html.

First, consider the source; look for an "about us" page. Check to determine who runs the site: Is it a branch of government, a university, a health organization, a hospital, or a business (especially such as a pharmaceutical manufacturer)? Focus on quality. Does the site have an editorial board? Is the information reviewed before it is posted? Be skeptical. Things that sound too good to be true often are. You want current, unbiased information based on research. Some of the information on these websites is reliable. Some of it is not. Some of the information is current. Some of it is not.

As you search online, you are likely to find websites for many health agencies and organizations that are not well-known. By answering the questions in the checklist below you should be able to find more information about these websites. A lot of these details can be found under the links on the site such as "About Us" or "Contact Us."

A CHECKLIST FOR ONLINE HEALTH INFORMATION

You can use the following checklist to assure that the health information you are reading online can be trusted.

- Can you easily identify the sponsor of the website?
- Is the funding source readily apparent?
- Do they clearly state their mission, their goal?
- Is there contact information indicating where the sponsor and/or the authors of the information can be reached?
- When was the information written? Is it current? New research findings can make a difference in making informed, effective choices. Check the home page to confirm when the website was last updated. Remember: older information isn't useless. Many websites provide an archive of older articles so readers may be able to acquire an in-depth knowledge of the topic they are researching.
- Who wrote the information? Authors and contributors should be identified. Their affiliation and any financial interest in the content should also be clear.
- Is the information reliable, authoritative? Such health information comes from scientific research that has been conducted in government, university, or private laboratories.

- Who reviews the information? Dependable websites will tell you where the health information came from and how it has been reviewed. Does the website have an editorial board? Are the board members experts in the subject you are researching?

- Is your privacy protected? Does the website clearly state a privacy policy? Read it carefully! If the website says something like: "We share information with companies that can provide you with products," that's a sign your information isn't private. NEVER give out your Social Security number. If you are asked for personal information, be sure to find out how the information is being used by contacting the website sponsor by phone, mail, or the "Contact Us" feature on the website. Look for information saying that a website has a "secure server" before purchasing anything online. Websites without such security may not protect your credit card or bank account information. As always, be careful when buying on the Internet.

- Does the website make claims that seem too good to be true? If the claims sound unbelievable they probably are! Beware of quick, miraculous cures that are promised. Be very skeptical about dramatic claims and testimonials.

As a caregiver, you will be well advised to read *Evaluating Health Information on the World Wide Web — A Hands-On Guide for Older Adults and Caregivers*. It can be downloaded at http://www.spry.org/sprys_work/education/Evaluat ingHealthInfo.html. This guide was prepared by The SPRY (Setting Priorities for Retirement Years) Foundation to help you evaluate the health information you find on the Internet. It is not designed to direct you to one site over another but rather to provide you with the tools needed to assess the reliability of any health web site. In describing the guide, the SPRY website states:

> The World Wide Web is becoming the source of health information for a growing number of older adults and their caregivers. With thousands of health-only web sites available, as well as thousands more sites with subsections on health topics, the choices are staggering. Any web user can become frustrated and confused when searching for specific health information, but these feelings can be even worse for people who may not have much web searching experience. You can see from our search results on 'health information' above that there is huge variation in what you might find when you search.
>
> Without experience, it can be difficult to structure a search to find exactly the information you want. And, even when you do an effective search, you may be confused about the nature of different health web sites. With all this variety, how can you find accurate, timely, understandable information on a specific topic with-

out spending hours online? Also, how can you feel confident about the quality of the information once you arrive at a promising site? We hope that this guide will help you to overcome these problems as you search for health information on the web.

How the Guide is Organized

- Part I: How Do You Find Reliable Health Web Sites?
- Part II: Evaluating the Content on Health Web Sites
- Part III: An Evaluation Checklist
- Part V: References and Contact Information
- Part IV: Health Web Site Issues of Privacy and Fraud

OTHER RESOURCES ON THE WEB

Health Compass

http://websites.afar.org/site/PageServer?pagename=HC_homepage

"Health Compass, developed by the American Federation for Aging Research and the Merck Institute of Aging & Health, offers older adults and their caregivers a way to search and evaluate health information on the Web in order to make informed healthcare decisions. A section on improving communication with medical personnel is also included."

This "how to" program is designed to help you better understand health information and research on aging. Health Compass shows you how to:

- find health information on the Internet
- evaluate the reliability of health information, product claims, and current research findings
- act on making informed decisions about your health

User's Guide to Finding and Evaluating Health Information on the Web

http://www.mlanet.org/resources/userguide.html

This resource from the Medical Library Association (MLA) states: "Millions of Americans search for health information on the Web every year. Whether the health information is needed for personal reasons or for a loved one, millions of health-related Web pages are viewed by millions of consumers. Sometimes the information found is just what was needed. Other searches end in frustration or retrieval of inaccurate, even dangerous, information."

"This guide outlines the collective wisdom of medical librarians who surf the Web every day to discover quality information in support of clinical and scientific decision making by doctors, scientists, and other health practitioners responsible for the nation's health. This guide is supported by the ... MLA, the library organization whose primary purpose is promoting quality information for improved health and whose members were the first to realize that not all health information on the Web is credible, timely, or safe."

Quackwatch

http://www.quackwatch.org

"Quackwatch, Inc. is a nonprofit corporation whose purpose is to combat health-related frauds, myths, fads, and fallacies. Its primary focus is on quackery-related information that is difficult or impossible to get elsewhere." The very interesting and informative site includes links to several online publications.

Who Cares: Sources of Information About Health Care Products and Services

http://www.ftc.gov/whocares

"With so many sources of health information at your fingertips—many of them online—it can be tough to tell fact from fiction, or useful health products and services from those that don't work or aren't safe."

"The Federal Trade Commission (FTC) has created this website to help you find reliable sources of information on health topics important to you, whether you're an older consumer or a family member, caregiver, or friend. You can:

- Find links to agencies and organizations that care about topics like generic drugs, hormone therapy, caregiving, surgery to improve vision, alternative medicine, hearing aids, Medicare fraud, and medical ID theft
- Learn how to spot misleading and deceptive claims
- Find out who you can contact to ask questions, enlist help, or speak up if you think a health product or service isn't living up to its promises."

FINAL NOTE ON THIS TOPIC

Among the best sources of health information is someone you can meet face-to-face — physicians and/or qualified healthcare providers. Otherwise, use your common sense and good judgment when evaluating health information online. There are websites on nearly every conceivable health topic and no rules overseeing the quality of the information. Consider everything before acting on any health information you find on the web. Don't count on any one website. If possible, check with several sources to confirm the accuracy of your results. Don't play doctor — consult one.

Online Resources

Metasites

These are websites that should be among the first caregivers should consult. They will provide a wealth of information as well as links to many other resources which will prove invaluable.

AARP — Caregiving

http://www.aarp.org/family/caregiving/

Topics on this site include:

- Caring for Parents
- Nursing Homes
- Alzheimer's Disease
- Independent Living
- Caregivers
- Assisted Living

There are also informative sections such as:

- Caregiving Tool Kit
  "Caregivers can access our extensive toolkit filled with interactive features, such as expert videos, calculators, and worksheets. It's a convenient stop for the information you need to care for your loved one or to volunteer to help out a friend."
- Get Organized!
  "Download our information form, which helps you identify where your most important papers are kept. This can save you added stress during an emergency."

- Long-Distance Caregiving
    "As a long-distance caregiver, you can take some steps to make the job more manageable."
- Screening Caregivers
    "If you're a caregiver, getting criminal background checks on other care providers and home health aides can help to protect older loved ones from mental, physical, and financial abuse."

Caregivers' Resources: U.S.A.gov

http://www.usa.gov/Citizen/Topics/Health/caregivers.shtml

Official information and services from the U.S. government. This extensive and authoritative site provides links to:

- Find Help Providing Care
- Government Benefits
- Legal Matters and End-of-Life Issues
- Long-Distance Caregiving
- Support for Caregivers.

Topics on these links include:

- Eldercare at Home
- Eldercare Locator
- Hospital Comparison
- Nursing Home Comparison
- *Long-Distance Caregivers Handbook* from the Family Caregiver Alliance
- Long-Distance Caregiving from the National Institute on Aging
- Caregiver Resources from Medicare.gov
- Caregiver Resources from MedlinePlus
- Caregivers of a Spouse or Partner
- Caring for an Aging Loved One
- Checklists and Forms for Caregivers
- National Caregivers Library
- National Family Caregiver Support Program
- Respite Care Locator
- Stress and Caregiving.

Eldercare at Home — A Comprehensive Online Guide for Family Caregivers

http://www.healthinaging.org/public_education/eldercare/1.xml

From The American Geriatrics Society Foundation for Health in Aging. "Written by experienced health professionals, the book is a tool for caregivers providing home care for an older person. Families are increasingly involved in caring for older adults who want to remain at home. Providing that care can be one of the most rewarding experiences of one's life. It can be one of the most challenging experiences as well. Family caregivers frequently have to deal with new, unfamiliar problems and learn new skills. They must do this in the context of strong emotional relationships. They must also involve the older person as much as possible in his or her own care. At the same time, family members need to take care of themselves so that they are able to provide the long-term care that is required and maintain their own quality of life. To meet these challenges, advice and guidance from experienced professionals can be important and helpful. The *Eldercare at Home* gives this guidance. The book gives clear, practical instructions for dealing with common caregiving problems and supports a problem-solving approach to managing care at home and working cooperatively with health professionals."

The book's 28 downloadable chapters include:

- Caregiving
- Incontinence
- Communication Problems
- Memory Problems
- Dementia
- Choosing a Nursing Home
- Advance Directives
- Dying At Home.

Family Caregiver Alliance — National Center on Caregiving — NCC

http://www.caregiver.org

"Established in 2001 as a program of Family Caregiver Alliance, the National Center on Caregiving (NCC) works to advance the development of high-quality, cost-effective policies and programs for caregivers in every state in the country. Uniting research, public policy and services, the NCC serves as a central source of information on caregiving and long-term care issues for policy makers, service providers, media, funders and family caregivers throughout the country."

Services include:

- "Family Care Navigator: a first-of-its-kind, state-by-state, online guide to help families in all 50 states locate government, nonprofit, and private caregiver support programs. The easy-to-use Navigator lists programs for family caregivers as well as resources for older or disabled adults living at home or in a residential facility.
- Caregiver Information & Assistance: personalized help to identify local resources and services for families, caregivers and providers nationwide, as well as publications on a wide array of topics.
- Research & Publications: NCC public policy briefs, Fact Sheets, monographs and research studies document current issues, caregiver needs, services and Best Practices. Our electronic newsletter, Caregiving PolicyDigest, highlights legislation, research, policy changes, events and new program developments."

Health and Aging Organizations

http://www.nia.nih.gov/HealthInformation/ResourceDirectory.htm

From the National Institute on Aging. This online, searchable database lists more than 300 national organizations that provide help to older people and their caregivers. Use the drop-down menu on the site to search subject areas for information on how to contact these organizations. The extensive list of organizations deal with such topics as:

- Adult Day Care
- Alzheimer's Disease
- Assisted Living
- Caregiving
- Communication Disorders
- Community Based
- Care Community Service
- Crisis Intervention
- Elder Abuse
- Incontinence
- Legal Issues

- Long Term Care
- Medical Care
- Medicare
- Respite Care
- Social Security
- Support Groups.

Medicare Caregiver Information

http://www.medicare.gov/caregivers/caregiving_exchange.asp

"This caregiver resource list includes some useful organizations available to help answer questions as a place to start your search for information. We've included only national organizations and many have extensive lists of additional resources." They include:

- About You, the Caregiver
- Message Boards, Discussion Groups, Forums and Blogs
- Caregiving Newsletters
- Tips, Facts and Checklists
- State Resources
- Elder Care
- End of Life
- Caregiver Stories
- Publications
- Housing Options
- Information for Professionals, Providers and Employers
- Other Federal Resources for Caregiving

MedicineNet.com — Caregiving

http://www.medicinenet.com/caregiving/article.htm

Topics include:

- What is a caregiver?
- Who are our nation's caregivers?
- What is caregiver stress?
- How can I tell if caregiving is putting too much stress on me?
- What can I do to prevent stress or relieve stress?

- What is respite care?
- What is the National Family Caregiver Support Program (NFCSP)?
- How can I find out about caregiving resources in my community?
- What kind of caregiver services can I find in my community?
- What kind of home care help is available?
- How will I pay for home health care?
- Who is eligible for Medicare home health care services?
- Will Medicaid help pay for home health care?

National Alliance for Caregiving — NAC

http://www.caregiving.org/

The National Alliance for Caregiving is dedicated to providing support to family caregivers and the professionals who help them and to increasing public awareness of issues facing family caregivers.

"Established in 1996, The National Alliance for Caregiving is a non-profit coalition of national organizations focusing on issues of family caregiving. Alliance members include grassroots organizations, professional associations, service organizations, disease-specific organizations, a government agency, and corporations. The Alliance was created to conduct research, do policy analysis, develop national programs, increase public awareness of family caregiving issues, work to strengthen state and local caregiving coalitions, and represent the U.S. caregiving community internationally. Recognizing that family caregivers provide important societal and financial contributions toward maintaining the well-being of those they care for, the Alliance's mission is to be the objective national resource on family caregiving with the goal of improving the quality of life for families and care recipients."

NAC publications for caregivers include:

- Family Care Resource Connection. This one-of-a-kind resource contains reviews and ratings of over 1,000 of the best books, videos, Web sites, and other materials on caregiving.
- *Care for the Family Caregiver: A Place to Start*
- *Resources for Caregivers — 2007 Edition*
- *Aging Parents & Common Sense Resource Directory*
- Family Caregiving 101, an online resource replete with quality information on how to deal with the challenges of caregiving. (See the entry in the list of resources for access information.)

National Care Planning Council: Long Term Care Link

http://www.longtermcarelink.net/

From the National Care Planning Council. "Long Term Care Link is one of the most comprehensive long term care sites on the internet. This non-commercial source of long term care information offers about 280 web pages which in turn can produce well over 2,000 pages of printed materials. Besides the in-depth information, I also offer you a free referral service to link you with long term care experts and advisors in your area."

National Council on Aging (NCOA))

http://www.ncoa.org/

"Improving the lives of older Americans" In the top bar click on "Promoting Independence & Dignity" to open a webpage with a list of links on various topics. Explore this informative website.

National Family Caregivers Association — NFCA

http://www.nfcacares.org

"The National Family Caregivers Association educates, supports, empowers and speaks up for the more than 50 million Americans who care for loved ones with a chronic illness or disability, or the frailties of old age. NFCA reaches across the boundaries of diagnoses, relationships and life stages to help transform family caregivers' lives by removing barriers to health and well being."

NFCA's core Caring Every Day messages are:

- Believe in Yourself.
- Protect Your Health.
- Reach Out for Help.
- Speak Up for Your Rights.

NFCA offers a virtual library of information and educational materials including:

- "Tips and Tools: NFCA's popular 10 Tips for Family Caregivers and How to Guides and other great Web site tools designed to help Family Caregivers.

- Agencies and Organizations: Find hundreds caregiving Web sites and resources for insurance, training, respite, disease-specific information and Medicare, etc.

- CCAN — Caregiver Community Action Network: In an effort to bring the NFCA's mission and support directly to family caregivers, a state network of dedicated volunteers has been created to provide vital information, education, and support.

- NFCA Publications: NFCA resource library offers essential caregiver educational materials.

- *Take Care Newsletter*: NFCA's quarterly newsletter written to provide members of NFCA with information, insight, support, and knowledge. Includes archive of all newsletters back to 2001.

- Health Care Information: This section has been created to provide you with information on specific diseases, conditions, and symptoms. The content has been provided to NFCA by sponsoring companies and organizations that have provided NFCA with an educational grants in return for the right to provide this information to you.

- Depression in Caregivers: Depression is significantly more common in family caregivers than in the rest of the population. This special section will teach you about major depression, direct you to a screening test and other depression resources, and give you ideas for coping with depression and the stress that can cause it or make it worse.

- Family Caregiving 101: The National Family Caregivers Association, (NFCA) in conjunction with the National Alliance of Caregivers, (the Alliance) created a powerful national campaign entitled: Family Caregiving: It's not all up to you to aid in educational services and support for family caregivers." (See the entry in Resources for additional information and the link to this publication.)

Net of Care

http://www.netofcare.org/

Information and resources for caregivers. Click on the link "Caregiver Resource Directory" which is described as "a practical guide that includes much of the information available on this site, while also offering a way to organize materials and information."

Topics/links include:

- tips for new caregivers
- stress
- financial and insurance assistance
- communicating with health care professionals
- managing symptoms at home
- handling medical emergencies
- goals of care
- DNR orders
- hospice
- coping with the emotional aspects of caregiving
- caring for patients with specific illnesses

Open Directory — Seniors

http://search.dmoz.org/cgi-bin/search?search=caregivers&all=yes&cs=UTF-8&cat= Society%2FPeople%2FGenerations_and_Age_Groups%2FSeniors

Links to over 500 sites on many topics, including senior health.

Resources for Caregivers

http://www.makoa.org/caregiver.htm

An extensive listing of links for caregivers. Categories include:

- Support for Caregivers
- Caregiving Resources
- Care Homes/Homecare
- Special Needs Trust
- Death and Dying

Resources for Caregivers: About.com

http://search.about.com/fullsearch.htm?terms=resources%20for%20caregivers

This site contains over 700 links on every conceivable topic of interest to caregivers.

Resources for Caregivers — MetLife

http://www.caregiving.org/pubs/brochures/resourcesforcaregivers07.pdf

"*Resources for Caregivers* was prepared to help individuals and families who have assumed the role of caregiver or anticipate future caregiving." A download-able 40-page brochure from MetLife.

Since You Care Guides

http://www.metlife.com/mmi/publications/since-you-care-guides/index.html?WT.ac=GN_mmi_publications_since-you-care-guides

A variety of guides from MetLife Mature Market Institute. These include:

- Adult Day Centers
- Alzheimer's Disease: Caregiving Challenges
- Becoming an Effective Advocate for Care
- Choosing an Assisted Living Facility
- Community Services
- Falls and Fall Prevention
- Family Caregiving
- Legal Matters
- Long Distance Caregiving
- Making the Nursing Home Choice
- Medications and the Older Adult
- Medicare and Medicaid Programs—The Basics
- Preventing Elder Abuse
- Resources for Caregivers
- Reaching for Tomorrow
- Understanding Home Care Agency Options

Strength for Caring

http://www.strengthforcaring.com/

"A place for caregivers." The Caregiver Initiative site from Johnson & Johnson. This award-winning website provides a wealth of information for caregivers on topics such as financial planning, legal issues, insurance and daily care. It includes links to other caregiver websites and the ability to download and print caregiving brochures from a variety of organizations. Caregivers will also find helpful worksheets and tips including a "Doctor's Office Visit Checklist" from the National Family Caregivers Association. In addition, the website has a list-ing of state-wide and local caregiving and healthcare resources as well as support information for each of the 50 states." Start with the link "Caregiver Manual." Topics/links in the manual include:

- About You
- Balancing Work & Family
- Stress Relief
- Support & Resources
- Food, Fitness, & Wellness
- Comfort & Relaxation
- Worksheets, Tips, & Facts
- Grief, Death, & Dying
- News & Events

suite101.com — Elderly Caregiving

http://www.suite101.com/articles.cfm/elderly_caregiving

Numerous articles on a variety of topics including:

- Caregiving Introduction
- Caring for Parents
- Caregiver Stress Signs
- Caregiver Feelings
- Long Distance Caregiving
- The Healthy Caregiver
- Depression in the Elderly
- Caregiver Burnout: For Family Members
- Communication Difficulties
- Caregiving Responsibilities

Your Caregiver's Handbook

http://www.seniormag.com/caregiverresources/handbook/index.htm

"A handbook for taking care of senior parents. This caregiver's handbook was created with the goal in mind to give caregivers an idea of what may lay ahead, but most importantly, a reality check on the situation at hand ... what is reasonable, and when too much is too much." FREE. Links to downloadable sections include:

- checklists
- list of needs
- types of available help
- caring for the caregiver
- personal care activities
- nutrition
- emotional well-being
- legal and financial affairs
- liability of care giving
- choosing a residential care facility

End of Life Issues

Advance Directives

http://www.nlm.nih.gov/medlineplus/advancedirectives.html

What kind of medical care would you want if you were too ill or traumatized to express your wishes? Advance directives — which include living wills and durable powers of attorney — are legal documents that allow you to convey your decisions about end-of-life care ahead of time. They provide a way for you to communicate your wishes to family, friends, and health care professionals, and to avoid confusion later on. A living will documents your wishes regarding interventions intended to sustain your life — what you desire, what you refuse. There are many issues to address, including:

- resuscitation
- dialysis
- tube feeding
- mechanical ventilation
- organ or tissue donation

A durable power of attorney for health care is a document that names your health care proxy. Your proxy is someone you trust to make health decisions if you are unable to do so.

This site from the National Library of Medicine has a number of links on both of these topics. It is a good place to start exploring the subjects. For a description of living wills and durable powers of attorney the reader is referred to questions 18 and 19 in Appendix B, *So Far Away: Twenty Questions for Long-Distance Caregivers.*

Advance Directives by State

http://www.noah-health.org/en/rights/endoflife/adforms.html

Links to download and print each state's advance directive form. It is essential that the individual preparing an advance directive use the form which is legal in their state. There is much more on this site relating each state's requirements.

Americans for Better Care of the Dying (ABCD)

http://www.abcd-caring.org/

"We can change what people face as they come to the end of life. Every dying person needs to be able to count on excellent care. Americans for Better Care of the Dying aims to improve end-of-life care by learning which social and political changes will lead to enduring, efficient, and effective programs. We work with the public, clinicians, policymakers, and other end-of-life organizations to make change happen."

Caring Connections

http://www.caringinfo.org/?gclid=COTo-sD-0Y0CFQISYQodaULbYQ

Caring Connections, a program of the National Hospice and Palliative Care Organization, is a national consumer and community engagement initiative to improve care at the end of life. It is supported by a grant from The Robert Wood Johnson Foundation.

Consumer's Tool Kit for Health Care Advance Planning

http://www.abanet.org/aging/toolkit/

A website of the American Bar Association Commission on Law and Aging. "Good advance planning for health care decisions is, in reality, a continuing conversation — about values, priorities, the meaning of one's life, and quality of life. To help you in this process, this tool kit contains a variety of self-help worksheets, suggestions, and resources. There are 10 tools in all, each clearly labeled and user-friendly. The tool kit does not create a formal advance directive for you. Instead, it helps you do the much harder job of discovering, clarifying, and communicating what is important to you in the face of serious illness."

Coping & Caring for Senior Citizens

http://www.seniors-site.com/coping/index.html

"Here we provide information on subjects that are sensitive for most of us. It is these topics that loved ones, significant others, and caregivers must necessarily cope with on occasion. For those who must deal with these circumstances we hope the information is helpful."

Topics Include:

- Coping with old age—taking care of yourself.
- How to treat senior citizens—as you would like to be treated.
- Communicating with people who are sick—suggestions that you might consider.
- Essential care for the sick and dying.
- Dealing with people who have a handicap—how to act and how not to act.
- Dealing with the severely injured—helping with a positive attitude.
- Learning to cope with chronic illness—suggestions for patients and for significant others.

Death and Dying—AARP

http://www.aarp.org/internetresources/

Forty-nine brief website descriptions including:

- End-of-Life Issues (advance directives, DNR orders, etc.)
- Funeral Practices
- Grief and Loss
- Hospice Care

EDELE

http://www.edeledata.org/search/home.html

"Are you a family member or individual looking for resources on death and dying? EDELE has probed the Internet and identified websites and web pages with useful data about decedents, dying and end-of-life experience. We offer several strategies to search our database of records. Each search returns a list of web pages and a brief description of the data found at each one."

End of Life — AARP

http://www.aarp.org/endoflife/

Topics include:

- Resources on end of life
- Advance directives
- Living wills
- Hospice care
- Talking about your final wishes
- Live your final days to the fullest

End-of Life Issues

http://www.usa.gov/Topics/Seniors/EndofLife.shtml

Official information and services from the U.S. government. Topics/links include:

- Coping with Loss
- Eldercare at Home
- Estate Planning and Wills
- Hospice Care
- Hospice Locator
- Living Wills and Advance Directives
- National Family Caregivers Support Program
- *Funerals — A Consumer Guide* (see entry below)

Funerals — A Consumer Guide

http://www.ftc.gov/bcp/edu/pubs/consumer/products/pro19.shtm

From the Federal Trade Commission. "When a loved one dies, grieving family members and friends often are confronted with dozens of decisions about the funeral — all of which must be made quickly and often under great emotional duress. What kind of funeral should it be? What funeral provider should you use? Should you bury or cremate the body, or donate it to science? What are you legally required to buy? What other arrangements should you plan? And, as callous as it may sound, how much is it all going to cost? Each year, Americans grapple with these and many other questions as they spend billions of dollars arranging more than 2 million funerals for family members and friends."

Gentle Endings

http://www.healthandage.com/html/min/gentle_endings/

"People are often woefully ill-prepared for death, even when there is adequate advanced warning. Gentle Endings aims to help by providing information for you and your loved ones about different aspects of dying. Items covered include grieving, hospice services, recommended reading, and links to useful sites." These links include:

- A guide to end of life care
- Understanding your emotions about grieving
- First step on the last journey
- Anxiety — the most misunderstood element in end-of-life care

Grief and Loss

http://www.aarp.org/griefandloss/

An AARP Web page. "A collection of resources, a community of care." Includes:

- Final details
- Funeral arrangements
- Ways parents can cope
- Helping grandchildren deal with grief
- On being alone — a guide for the newly widowed

Hospice Foundation of America

www.hospicefoundation.org

The Foundation promotes hospice care and educates professionals and families about issues related to caregiving, terminal illness, loss, and bereavement.

Hospice Net

http://www.hospicenet.org/

Click on the link "Caregivers" in the sidebar to access these topics:

- How to Be a Supportive Caregiver
- Preparing for Approaching Death
- Helping a Friend Who Is Dying
- Hard Choices for Loving People
- Family and Medical Leave Act
- Hiring In-home Health
- The Caregiver's Journey Through Hospice
- Keeping Watch
- Saying Good-bye

National Hospice and Palliative Care Organization (NHPCO)

http://www.nhpco.org

"The National Hospice and Palliative Care Organization is the largest non-profit membership organization representing hospice and palliative care programs and professionals in the United States. The organization is committed to improving end of life care and expanding access to hospice care with the goal of profoundly enhancing the quality of life for people dying in America and that of their loved ones."

"Considered to be the model for quality, compassionate care at the end of life, hospice care involves a team-oriented approach of expert medical care, pain management, and emotional and spiritual support expressly tailored to the patient's wishes. Emotional and spiritual support also is extended to the family and loved ones. Generally, this care is provided in the patient's home or in a home-like setting operated by a hospice program. Medicare, private health insurance, and Medicaid in most states cover hospice care for patients who meet certain criteria."

Publications, fact sheets, and website resources are available on topics including how to find and evaluate hospice services.

Put It in Writing

http://www.putitinwriting.org/putitinwriting_app/index.jsp

"An advance directive is your life on your terms. Whether you're 18 or 80, documenting your wishes today means your family won't have to make heart-wrenching decisions later. To help patients, families and the hospitals that serve them, the American Hospital Association (AHA), with the cooperation of other organizations, has compiled key resources to enhance educational efforts and raise awareness around this important issue."

Download the 10-page brochure (PDF) *Put It in Writing* which provides basic facts about advance directives and encourages patients to explore their preferences for care at the end of life. There also links to a glossary of terms, and a wallet ID card that alerts healthcare workers that patients have talked to their family about advance directives and provides contact names and numbers. Simply print, then fill out the card and carry it in your wallet. This site also has a link to sources of state-specific advance directives.

10 Legal Myths About Advance Medical Directives
http://www.abanet.org/aging/myths.html

A resource from the American Bar Association Commission on Legal Problems of the Elderly. The myths include:

- "Everyone should have a Living Will."
- "An Advance Directive means 'Don't treat.'"
- "I need a lawyer to create an Advance Directive."
- "Advance Directives are a legal tool for old people."

Ultimate Concerns— Death and Dying
http://www.seniors-site.com/ultimate/index.html

"These pages on Seniors-Site are dedicated to providing information on a most difficult subject — death. Yet death is an inevitable. We suggest you become acquainted with the information provided especially if you are responsible for making life & death decisions for others." Topics include: life-sustaining decisions, hospice care, recording last wishes, and funeral planning. The site also includes links to a number of other websites on death and dying.

U.S. Living Will Registry
http://www.uslivingwillregistry.com

The Registry stores all types of advance directives—living wills, health care proxies, health care powers of attorney, as well as organ donor information.

Legal Issues

Compliance Assistance — Family and Medical Leave Act (FMLA)

http://www.dol.gov/esa/whd/fmla/

For the Employment Guide — Family and Medical Leave go to: http://www.dol.gov/compliance/guide/fmla.htm

Synopsis of the Law: Covered employers must grant an eligible employee up to a total of 12 workweeks of unpaid leave during any 12-month period for one or more of the following reasons:

- to care for an immediate family member (spouse, child, or parent) with a serious health condition
- for the birth and care of the newborn child of the employee
- for placement with the employee of a son or daughter for adoption or foster care
- to take medical leave when the employee is unable to work because of a serious health condition

Consumer Protection for Seniors

http://www.usa.gov/Topics/Seniors/Consumer.shtml

Official information and services from the U.S. government. Topics/links include:

- Advocates for Residents of Nursing Homes, by State
- Commission on Legal Problems of the Elderly
- *Consumer Action Handbook*
- Consumer Protection Offices
- Elder Rights and Resources
- Federal Trade Commission Consumer Protection Page
- Financial Crimes Against the Elderly
- Health Fraud and the Elderly
- H.E.L.P. — Helping People Meet Aging-Related Legal and Care Challenges
- Long Term Care Ombudsman Program (Administration on Aging)
- Medicare and Medicaid: Protection Against Fraud

- Preventing Fraud and Abuse (Administration on Aging)
- Social Security — Protect Your Social Security Number

Elder Abuse: Laws

http://elder-law.lawyers.com/Elder-Abuse.html

Website of lawyers.com. "While all 50 states have enacted laws that address the problem of elder abuse and neglect, the laws are not uniform. Under federal law, an older individual is a person who is 60 years of age and older. Many states follow the federal law and use the age of 60 as the baseline age for elderly individuals. Some state laws recognize that protected older individuals are 65 years of age and older and/or disabled."

Elder Law and Legal Resources on the Web

http://www.seniorlaw.com/resource.htm

Several pages of hyperlinks to legal resources, including nine listings of links relevant to senior citizens.

Legal Issues Important to Senior Citizens

http://www.seniors-site.com/legalm/index.html

Topics include:

- Legal help for senior citizens
- How to select a lawyer
- Organizing your important records
- Estate planning
- Probate
- Guardianship
- Life support wishes including living wills, and durable powers of attorney

National Center on Elder Abuse (NCEA)

http://www.ncea.aoa.gov/ncearoot/Main_Site/index.aspx

"If you're a caregiver: Most families do not abuse, neglect, or exploit older loved ones, nor do paid caregivers. If you are having a difficult time, there are resources to help." Site includes numerous links to online resources, including useful publications such as "Preventing Stress from Becoming Harmful: A Guide for Caregivers," "Where to Report Nursing Home Abuse," "Preventing Elder Abuse by Family Caregivers," and "Preventing Elder Abuse by In-Home Helpers."

Medical and Health Care

Age Pages

http://www.niapublications.org/shopdisplayproducts.asp?cat=All

These are brief articles on various categories relating to aging that are published by the National Institutes on Aging (NIA). Use this page to search, view, and order these publications and other materials. Most are free. Sale publications can be purchased with a credit card or online check. Free shipping on all orders to the U.S. and Canada. In January 2010 the list of Age Pages included:

- A Good Night's Sleep
- Aging and Your Eyes
- Arthritis Advice
- Choosing a Doctor
- Constipation
- Crime and Older People
- Diabetes in Older People — A Disease You Can Manage
- Dietary Supplements — More Is Not Always Better
- Exercise — Getting Fit for Life
- Foot Care
- Forgetfulness — It's Not Always What You Think
- Getting Your Affairs in Order
- Health Quackery — Spotting Health Scams
- Hearing Loss
- High Blood Pressure
- Hyperthermia — Too Hot for Your Health
- Hypothermia — A Cold Weather Hazard
- Life Extension — Science Fact or Science Fiction
- Long Term Care — Choosing the Right Place
- Medicines — Use Them Safely

- Older Drivers
- Preventing Falls & Fractures
- Prostate Problems
- Sexuality in Later Life
- Skin Care and Aging
- Stroke — Prevention and Treatment
- Urinary Incontinence

Alzheimer's Association

www.alz.org

The Alzheimer's Association is a national, nonprofit association with a network of local chapters that provide education and support for people diagnosed with Alzheimer's disease, their families, and caregivers. The Association also supports research on AD.

Alzheimer's Disease Education and Referral (ADEAR) Center

www.nia.nih.gov/Alzheimers

A service of the National Institute on Aging (NIA), the ADEAR Center offers information and publications for families, caregivers, and professionals on diagnosis, treatment, patient care, caregiver needs, long-term care, education and training, and research related to AD. Staff members answer telephone, email, and written requests and make referrals to local and national resources. The ADEAR website offers free, online publications in English and Spanish; email alert and online Connections newsletter subscriptions; an AD clinical trials database; the AD Library database; and more.

Alzheimer's Foundation of America

www.alzfdn.org

The Alzheimer's Foundation of America provides care and services to individuals confronting dementia and to their caregivers and families through member organizations dedicated to improving quality of life. Services include a toll-free hotline, consumer publications and other educational materials, and conferences and workshops.

Centers for Medicare and Medicaid Services (CMS)

http://cms.hhs.gov

The Centers for Medicare & Medicaid Services is a federal agency within the U.S. Department of Health and Human Services. Click on the link "About CMS" for detailed information. The CMS site provides information for consumers and professionals and is divided into "Consumer Information" and "Professional/Technical Information." A number of publications are available, many of them available online at this site. The website also has a search engine.

Deciphering Medspeak

http://www.mlanet.org/resources/medspeak/topten.html

"The Medical Library Association finds the following web sites particularly useful (sites are listed in alphabetical, NOT ranked, order.)" Sites/links include:

- Cancer.gov
- Centers for Disease Control and Prevention (CDC)
- familydoctor.org
- healthfinder
- HIV InSite
- Mayo Clinic

FamilyDoctor.org.

http://familydoctor.org/online/famdocen/home/seniors.html

From the American Academy of Family Physicians (AAFP): "The American Academy of Family Physicians is a national association of doctors in family practice which offers education and information on health care and disease prevention. The AAFP's very comprehensive and informative website offers free fact sheets on specific diseases, questions and answers about common health issues, self-care flow charts, and databases on drugs and drug reactions." Healthcare topics for senior citizens include:

- Active Living
- Mental Health
- Staying Healthy
- End-of-Life Care

- Seniors and Medicines
- Managing Your Medical Care
- Common Conditions in Older Adults

Federal Health Websites of Interest to Older Adults
http://nihseniorhealth.gov/toolkit/toolkitfiles/html/Module_9.html

Health issues are a vital concern for older adults, and surveys show that most of those who go online search for health and medical information. However, since only 34 percent of people age 65 and older are online, the majority of older adults are missing out on valuable health information. To broaden the numbers of older adults able to search for and find reliable health information online, the National Institute on Aging (NIA) has developed a free training curriculum for those who teach and work with older adults. This list of websites was derived from the curriculum.

1. Administration on Aging (AOA)
   www.aoa.gov
     AOA plans and delivers home and community-based services to older adults and their caregivers.
2. Centers for Disease Control and Prevention (CDC)
   www.cdc.gov
     The CDC promotes health and quality of life by preventing and controlling disease, injury, and disability.
3. Centers for Medicare and Medicaid Services (CMS)
   www.cms.gov
     CMS administers Medicare and Medicaid. Medicare is the federal health insurance program for people age 65 and older and for people with disabilities. Medicaid is a joint federal-state program that provides health insurance coverage to low-income people including children, older adults, and people with disabilities.
4. Clinical Trials.gov
   www.clinicaltrials.gov
     This website contains information about clinical trials sponsored by the National Institutes of Health, other federal agencies, and private industry. Clinical trials are research studies with human volunteers to determine if a drug, treatment, or therapy is safe and effective.
5. Department of Health and Human Services
   www.dhhs.gov

The Department of Health and Human Services is the U.S. government's principal agency for protecting the health of all Americans and providing essential human services.

6. Food and Drug Administration (FDA)
www.fda.gov
The FDA regulates the safety and effectiveness of food products, additives, drugs, medical devices, and cosmetics.

7. healthfinder.gov
www.healthfinder.gov
This website features consumer health information from government agencies, nonprofit organizations, and universities.

8. MedlinePlus.gov
www.medlineplus.gov
This website from the National Library of Medicine features health information on more than 700 topics for patients, families, and the public.

9. National Institute on Aging (NIA)
www.nia.nih.gov
NIA, part of the National Institutes of Health, leads the federal effort supporting and conducting research on aging and the medical, social, and behavioral issues of older people.

10. National Institutes of Health (NIH)
www.nih.gov
NIH, part of the U.S. Department of Health and Human Services, is the primary federal agency conducting and supporting medical research. It includes 27 Institutes and Centers whose collective goal is to investigate ways to prevent, treat, and cure common and rare diseases.

11. NIHSeniorHealth.gov
www.nihseniorhealth.gov
This senior-friendly website from the National Institutes of Health features health and wellness information for older adults.

Health — FirstGov for Seniors

http://www.firstgov.gov/Topics/Seniors.shtml#vgn-health-vgn

This is an essential site for caregivers. The topics addressed at this authoritative and comprehensive federal government website include:

- Aging and Injury
- Alzheimer's Disease
- Arthritis and Rheumatic Diseases
- Caregivers
- Costs of Fall Injuries Among Older Adults
- Disability Resources
- Eldercare Locator
- Environmental Health of Older Adults
- Exercise for Older Adults
- Falls and Hip Fractures Among Older Adults
- Falls in Nursing Homes
- Food Safety for Seniors
- Funerals—A Consumer Guide
- Growing Older, Eating Better
- Health Agencies by State
- Health Information for Older Adults
- Health Issues for Seniors
- Hospice Care
- Hospice Locator
- How to Keep a Healthy Heart
- Medicaid
- Medicare
- Medicare Card Replacement
- Medicare Plan Comparison
- Nursing Home Comparison
- Nutrition and Aging
- Nutrition and Your Health
- Older Adult Drivers
- Older Adults and Injuries
- Prescription Drug Assistance
- Private Duty Home Care
- SeniorHealth.gov
- Shattering the Myths of Old Age
- State Mental Health Resources
- Young at Heart: Tips for Older Adults

Health for Seniors

http://www.usa.gov/Topics/Seniors/Health.shtml

Official information and services from the U.S. government. Numerous topics/links include:

- Disease, Injury, and Abuse
- Doctors and Health Care Facilities
- Medicare and Medicaid

Health Information for Older Adults

http://www.cdc.gov/aging/info.htm#8

Information from the CDC — topics/links include:

- Health-Related Behaviors
- Chronic Diseases
- Mental Health
- Infectious Diseases
- Immunizations for Adults
- Injuries Among Older Adults
- Medicare

Health Links— Aging/Elder Care (FCIC)

http://www.pueblo.gsa.gov/links/he37links.htm

Links to government and private sources from the Federal Citizen Information Center.

healthfinder.gov

http://www.healthfinder.gov

"[H]ealthfinder is an award-winning federal website for consumers, developed by the U.S. Department of Health and Human Services together with other federal agencies. Since 1997, healthfinder has been recognized as a key resource for finding the best government and nonprofit health and human services information on the Internet." "Health A to Z" is an encyclopedia of over 1,600 health topics from the most trusted sources.

HealthVault: Microsoft

http://www.healthvault.com/

"Like other Web-based personal health records, Microsoft's HealthVault is free and will allow consumers to store medical information—such as vaccination dates and X-rays—and share what they wish with physicians and relatives of their choosing." Microsoft asserts:

1. The Microsoft HealthVault record you create is controlled by you.
2. You decide what goes into your HealthVault record.
3. You decide who can see and use your information on a case-by-case basis.
4. We do not use your health information for commercial purposes unless we ask and you clearly tell us we may.

Hospital Compare

http://www.hospitalcompare.hhs.gov/Hospital/Search/Welcome.asp?version=default&browser=IE%7C7%7CWinXP&language=English&defaultstatus=0&pagelist=Home

From the Department of Health and Human Services. "Hospital Compare displays rates for Process of Care measures that show how often hospitals provide some of the care that is recommended for patients being treated for a heart attack, heart failure or pneumonia, or patients having surgery. Hospitals voluntarily submit data from their medical records about the treatments their adult patients receive for these conditions, including patients with Medicare and those who do not have Medicare."

Hospital Discharge Planning: Helping Family Caregivers Through the Process

http://www.caregiving.org/pubs/brochures/DischargePlanner.pdf

This 20 page booklet is "intended to make discharge planning a little smoother by informing family caregivers of what to expect and by giving you, the discharge planner, some insights about the family's perspective."

MedLinePlus: Seniors' Health

http://www.nlm.nih.gov/medlineplus/seniorshealth.html

Webpage from the National Library of Medicine with extensive links relevant to the elderly and their caregivers. "Americans are living longer than ever before. Many seniors live active and healthy lives. But there's no getting around one thing: as we age, our bodies and minds change. There are things you can do to stay healthy and active as you age. Eating a balanced diet, keeping mind and body active, not smoking, getting regular checkups, and practicing safety habits at home and in the car will help you make the most of life."

MUST — Medication Use Safety Training for Seniors

http://www.mustforseniors.org/index.jsp

"The Medication Use Safety Training for Seniors (MUST) program is designed as an interactive, national initiative to promote safe and appropriate medicine use by enabling older adults to avoid medication misuse, recognize and manage common side effects, and improve medicine use knowledge, attitudes, and skills to avoid medication errors.

MUST for Senior can be offered to community-based, ambulatory older adults. Older individuals and family caregivers are also encouraged to use this site and to participate in the program by viewing the online PowerPoint presentation, video clips and other program messages and materials."

National Association for Continence

http://www.nafc.org

"The National Association for Continence is a national, private, nonprofit organization dedicated to improving the quality of life of people with incontinence. NAFC's purpose is to be the leading source for public education and advocacy about the causes, prevention, diagnosis, treatments, and management alternatives for incontinence."

The Association provides a nationwide referral service for consumers and professionals. They also offer educational information and materials, such as pamphlets and audiovisual materials for the general public and health care professionals.

National Council on Patient Information and Education (NCPIE)

http://www.talkaboutrx.org/

"The National Council on Patient Information and Education is a coalition of over 125 diverse organizations whose mission is to stimulate and improve communication of information on appropriate medicine use to consumers and healthcare professionals. NCPIE is the nation's leading authority for informing the general public and health care professionals on safe medicine use through better communication. Better medicine communication can lead to better health outcomes and improved quality of life."

National Institute of Mental Health (NIMH)

http://www.nimh.nih.gov

The National Institute of Mental Health is one of twenty-seven components of the National Institutes of Health (NIH), the federal government's principal biomedical and behavioral research agency. NIH is part of the U.S. Department of Health and Human Services.

"The NIMH mission is to reduce the burden of mental illness and behavioral disorders through research on mind, brain, and behavior. This public health mandate demands that we harness powerful scientific tools to achieve better understanding, treatment, and eventually, prevention of these disabling conditions that affect millions of Americans."

Contact NIMH for information on mental health and aging. NIMH responds to information requests from the public, clinicians, and the scientific community with a variety of printed materials on such disorders as depression, seasonal affective disorder (SAD), Alzheimer's disease, and suicide. A list of publications, including those in Spanish, is available.

NIHSeniorHealth

http://nihseniorhealth.gov/

"NIHSeniorHealth makes aging-related health information easily accessible for family members and friends seeking reliable, easy to understand online health information. This site was developed by the National Institute on Aging (NIA) and the National Library of Medicine (NLM) both part of the National Institutes of Health (NIH).

NIHSeniorHealth features authoritative and up-to-date health information from Institutes and Centers at NIH. In addition, the American Geriatrics Society provides expert and independent review of some of the material found on this web site. Each health topic includes general background information, open-captioned videos, quizzes and frequently asked questions (FAQs). New topics are added to the site on a regular basis.

The web site's senior-friendly features include large print, short, easy-to-read segments of information and simple navigation. A 'talking' function reads the text aloud and special buttons to enlarge the text or turn on high contrast make text more readable." An excellent resource.

Partnership for Prescription Assistance

www.pparx.org

This program helps qualified people who lack prescription coverage to get needed medicines.

"Physical Activity and Health: Older Adults"

http://www.cdc.gov/nccdphp/sgr/olderad.htm

A Fact Sheet from the CDC. Includes "Key Messages," "Facts," "Benefits of Physical Activity," "What Communities Can Do." The site confirms that:

- The loss of strength and stamina attributed to aging is in part caused by reduced physical activity.
- Social support from family and friends has been consistently and positively related to regular physical activity.
- Older adults, both male and female, can benefit from regular physical activity.
- Physical activity need not be strenuous to achieve health benefits.
- Older adults can obtain significant health benefits with a moderate amount of physical activity, preferably daily.

Seniors' Health Issues-MedlinePlus

http://www.nlm.nih.gov/medlineplus/seniorshealthissues.html

"Americans are living longer than ever before. Many seniors live active and healthy lives. But there's no getting around one thing: as we age, our bodies and minds change. There are things you can do to stay healthy and active as you age. Eating a balanced diet, keeping mind and body active, not smoking, getting regular checkups, and practicing safety habits at home and in the car will help you make the most of life." Includes an exhaustive list of links on many topics relevant to healthcare of the elderly

"Talking with Your Doctor: A Guide for Older People"

http://www.niapublications.org/pubs/talking/index.asp

A 48-page booklet from the National Institute on Aging with numerous links to health and fitness topics, and health care organizations. "How well you and your doctor talk to each other is one of the most important parts of getting good health care. A good patient-doctor relationship is a partnership. You and your doctor can work as a team, along with nurses, physician assistants, pharmacists, and other health care providers. Taking an active role in your health care puts the responsibility for good communication on both you and your doctor. This is especially important for older people who may have more health conditions and treatments to discuss with the health care team."

This popular booklet provides several helpful worksheets, and offers many tips and suggestions, including:

- Choosing a doctor you can talk to.
- Getting ready for an appointment.
- Giving and getting information.
- Discussing sensitive subjects.
- Involving family and friends.

Training Guide from the National Institute on Aging Helps Older Adults Find Health Information Online

http://nihseniorhealth.gov/toolkit/toolkit.html

Health issues are a vital concern for older adults, and surveys show that most of those who go online search for health and medical information. However, since only 34 percent of people age 65 and older are online, the majority of older adults are missing out on valuable health information. To broaden the numbers of older adults able to search for and find reliable health information online, the National Institute on Aging (NIA) has developed a free training curriculum for those who teach and work with older adults. This Toolkit for Trainers is now available on NIHSeniorHealth.gov, a senior-friendly Web site developed by the NIA and the National Library of Medicine (NLM), components of the National Institutes of Health (NIH).

The Toolkit for Trainers is a resource developed by the National Institute on Aging. Use these free, easy-to-use training materials to help older adults find reliable, up-to-date online health information on their own. The training features two websites from the National Institutes of Health — NIHSeniorHealth.gov and MedlinePlus.gov. Trainers can use the toolkit with beginning and intermediate students of the Web.

Residential or Housing

AgeNet Eldercare Network

http://www.caregivers.com

"We are a free referral service helping families find nursing homes, assisted living, Alzheimer's care, retirement communities, home care, and other senior care options."

American Association of Homes and Services for the Aging

http://www.aahsa.org

This trade association for not-for-profit nursing homes, continuing care retirement communities, assisted living, senior housing facilities, and community service organizations offers information for consumers and families.

HIP Housing: Home Sharing

http://www.hiphousing.org/programs/sharing.html

"Home Sharing is a living arrangement in which two or more unrelated people share a home or apartment. Each has his/her private room and shares the common living areas. HIP Housing can facilitate two types of home sharing arrangements-rent or service exchange. In a match arrangement, a home provider is matched with a home seeker who pays rent. A service exchange, often involving seniors, entails a home seeker who agrees to provide services in lieu of rent."

Homeshare International

http://homeshare.org/default.aspx

"Homesharing is a simple idea. A householder offers accommodation to a homesharer in exchange for an agreed level of support. The support needed may be help with the household tasks, or it may be financial support, or a combination of both. Homeshare is essentially an exchange that recognizes that two people have needs and something to offer."

Homesharing

http://www.opm.gov/Employment_and_Benefits/WorkLife/OfficialDocuments/hand books guides/ElderCareResources/elder06.asp

A site from the U.S. Office of Personnel Management (OPM). "As an alternative to moving into your home, your parent may want to consider sharing their home with others, moving into someone else's home, or finding a new house that can accommodate them and several other people. Shared households can be arranged either by sharing expenses or by exchanging services for rent. For example, a homebound homeowner might prefer having someone do housework, shopping, yard work, or other errands in exchange for free lodging. This sort of arrangement should be put in writing, so there are no misunderstandings later."

Housing for Seniors: USA.gov

http://www.usa.gov/Topics/Seniors/Housing.shtml

This site contains links to:

- Administration on Aging — Housing
- Advocates for Residents of Nursing Homes, by State
- American Association of Homes and Services for the Aging
- Eldercare at Home
- Eldercare Locator
- Foreclosure Resources
- Homelessness
- Housing for Persons with Disabilities
- Housing Information for Seniors
- Nursing Home Comparison
- Reverse Mortgages for Seniors

National Aging in Place Council (NAIPC)

http://www.naipc.org/

"The National Aging in Place Council is a membership organization founded on the belief that an overwhelming majority of older Americans want to remain in their homes for as long as possible, but lack awareness of home and community-based services that make independent living possible. NAIPC has created a national forum for individuals from the aging, healthcare, financial services, legal, design and building sectors to work together to help meet the needs of our growing aging population, so they can continue living in the housing of their choice." Click in the links "Resource Directory" and "A Guide to Aging in Place" in the sidebar of the website.

National Home Share Resource Center

http://www.nationalsharedhousing.org/

The National Home Share Resource Center offers a nationwide directory of local organizations that sponsor home share programs. The basic concept is that an older person provides free housing in exchange for free care.

National Resource Center on Supportive Housing & Home Modifications

http://www.homemods.org

The National Resource Center on Supportive Housing and Home Modification is a university-based, nonprofit organization dedicated to promoting aging in place and independent living for persons of all ages and abilities. Contact the center for information on government-assisted housing, assisted living policies, home modifications for older people, training and education courses, and technical assistance. Publications and fact sheets are available.

Nursing Home Compare — Medicare

http://www.medicare.gov/default.asp

Click on the link on the right sidebar "Compare Nursing Homes in Your Area." "The primary purpose of this tool is to provide detailed information about the past performance of every Medicare and Medicaid certified nursing home in the country."

Senior Housing: Glossary

http://seniorliving.about.com/od/housingoptions/a/housingglossary.htm

A website from About.com lists commonly used terms for senior housing and care options.

U.S. Department of Housing and Urban Development (HUD))

http://www.hud.gov/groups/seniors.cfm

"Looking for housing options for yourself, an aging parent, relative, or friend? Do some research first to determine what kind of assistance or living arrangement you need; what your health insurance might cover; and what you can afford. Then check here for financial assistance resources and guides for making the right choice. Talk to a HUD-approved housing counselor [hyperlink on the website] if you have questions about your situation."

General

AARP — Caregivers Resource Center

http://www.aarp.org/family/caregiving/cg.resource.center

Caregiving checklists including:

- In-Home Care Agency: What to Ask
- Home Safety Checklist
- Preventing Falls Checklist
- Assisted Living: What to Ask
- Nursing Homes: What to Ask
- Hospice: What to Ask
- Dealing with Pain: What to Ask

AARP — Caregiving in the U.S. 2009

http://www.aarp.org/research/surveys/care/ltc/hc/articles/caregiving.09.html or
http://www.caregiving.org

Published in November 2009 by AARP, in collaboration with The National Alliance for Caregiving, and funded by the MetLife Foundation, the study is described as: "the most comprehensive examination to date of caregiving in America." The site provide these links:

- Full Report (PDF)
- Executive Summary (PDF)
- Caring for Someone Age 50+: Full Report (PDF)
- Caring for Someone Age 50+: Executive Summary (PDF)

AARP — Internet Resources on Aging

http://www.aarp.org/internetresources/

"Browse or search AARP's database on Internet resources, and link to more than 900 of the best sites for people age 50+."

Agencies and Organizations

http://www.thefamilycaregiver.org/caregiving_resources/agencies_and_organizations.
cfm

"A listing of links to agencies and organizations that are valuable resources for you to receive information, support and assistance — whether you are a family caregiver, a professional caregiver, or looking for additional information on issues related to family caregiving."

AgeNet

http://www.agenet.com/

"Solutions for Better Aging." Topics include health, drugs, legal, insurance, financial, caregiver, housing. Review the sidebar on the right of the webpage for links to:

- Eldercare locator
- Caregiver tools
- Ask the experts

This site is a resource for anyone seeking information about the social, emotional, and physical concerns of the elderly and their caregivers. There are a number of online articles on various topics which the reader can download and print.

Aging

http://www.hhs.gov/aging/index.shtml#caregivers

A website of the U.S. Department of Health and Human Services. Topics/ links include:

- Caregivers
- Data & Statistics
- Diseases & Conditions
- HHS & Other U.S. Government Agencies
- Hospitals, Nursing Homes, & Other Facilities
- Medicare & Medicaid
- Safety & Wellness
- Resources for Older People

Aging Initiative

http://www.epa.gov/aging/index.htm

From the U.S. Environmental Protection Agency. The website provides a wealth of information about the Agency's efforts to protect the environmental health of older persons. "Due to the normal aging process, even older persons in good health may experience increased health risks from exposures to environmental pollutants. As we age, our bodies are more susceptible to hazards from the environment which may worsen chronic or life threatening conditions." Among the many topics/links are:

- Age Healthier, Breathe Easier
- Building Healthy Communities for Active Aging
- Diabetes and Environmental Hazards
- Effective Control of Household Pests
- Environmental Hazards Weigh Heavy on the Heart
- "It's Too Darn Hot"—Planning for Excessive Heat
- Water Works

Aging Issues

http://www.helpguide.org

Articles and resources from Helpguide on aging issues and elder care. Clink on the link "Seniors and Aging" in the right sidebar.

Aging Parents and Common Sense: A Directory of Resources for You and Your Parents

http://www.caregiving.org/pubs/brochures/Aging%20Parent-Directory_5thEd.pdf

A publication from the NAC. This booklet is part of the AXA Equitable Consumer Insight Series created to educate and help the public understand the financial issues that may impact their lives. "At AXA, we are committed to giving our clients the tools to help them make the financial decisions that are right for them." 37 pages, PDF.

The resources provided in this directory are alphabetized within the following categories:

- general
- financial

- health
- legal
- housing

Aging Parents and Elder Care

http://www.aging-parents-and-elder-care.com

"An in-depth guide to caring for your elderly loved one. Helping people overcome the challenges of elder care. A guide to caring for your elderly loved one. Caring for an aging parent, elderly spouse, domestic partner or close friend presents tough challenges— especially when a crisis hits and the responsibilities of elder care descend upon you suddenly."

Aging Under the Microscope

http://www.nia.nih.gov/HealthInformation/Publications/AgingUndertheMicroscope/

"The study of aging is not what it used to be. Gerontology was a young science when Congress created the National Institute on Aging (NIA) in 1974 as part of the National Institutes of Health (NIH). At that time, theories of aging abounded, but data was scant. Gerontology lacked, or was just in the early stages of developing, ways to explore the fundamentals of the aging process. Knowledge of aging clustered around specific diseases associated with advancing age; indeed the notion that aging equated with decline and illness was widespread." 56 pages, PDF.

AGIS

http://www.agis.com/

AGIS offers a wealth of information for caregivers that will be extremely helpful. Topics/links on this site include:

- Caregiving Overview (See the entry which follows.)
- Find Facilities & Services
- Checklists
- Connect with Others
- Paying for Care
- Mental & Physical Health
- Caring for Yourself

Click on the link "More Topics" for a very extensive list.

Alzheimer's Association

http://www.alz.org/index.asp

The Alzheimer's Association offers information and supportive services to families and individuals dealing with Alzheimer's disease. Download the "Caregiver's Guide." The guide provides information on legal and financial planning, day-to-day care, hygiene and personal care, choosing health care providers and facilities, coping.

Alzheimer's Disease Education and Referral (ADEAR)

http://www.nia.nih.gov/Alzheimers/

ADEAR provides information to patients, families and professionals. The Center's website will help you find current, comprehensive Alzheimer's disease information and resources from the National Institute on Aging (NIA).

American Society on Aging (ASA)

http://www.asaging.org/index.cfm

"The largest organization of multidisciplinary professionals in the field of aging. Our resources, publications, and educational opportunities are geared to enhance the knowledge and skills of people working with older adults and their families."

ARCH National Respite Network and Resource Center

www.archrespite.org

This national center provides resources and information, including a respite locator program, technical assistance to state organizations, and an information clearinghouse.

Assisted Living Federation of America

http://www.alfa.org

Assisted Living Federation of America can help you search out residences by city, sate, or specific needs such as Alzheimer's.

BenefitsCheckUp

http://www.benefitscheckup.org

Developed and maintained by The National Council on Aging (NCOA), BenefitsCheckUp is the nation's most comprehensive Web-based service to screen for benefits programs for seniors with limited income and resources.

BenefitsCheckUp is a free service and is completely confidential. It does not require the user's name, address, phone number, Social Security number, or any other information that could be used to identify you. (Note, this service is provided by a private, nonprofit organization; it is neither a Federal Government site nor an official determination of eligibility.) For this, see the entry "GovBenefits."

Beverly Foundation

http://www.beverlyfoundation.org

"The Beverly Foundation's mission is to enhance the quality of life of the years that have been added to life, thus bettering the health and well being of older adults and that of their caregivers, and their families." It is an independent operating foundation. The program emphasizes research, demonstration, and education efforts that contribute to the ability of older adults to continue living in the community as long as possible. In keeping with its mission, the Foundation targets the audience of professionals, caregivers, family members and seniors themselves.

Care for Caregivers

http://www.eldernet.com/caregive.htm

Links to various support groups and resources for those involved with the long term care of a loved one.

Care for the Family Caregiver — A Place to Start

http://www.caregiving.org/pubs/brochures/CFC.pdf

This 46 page brochure discusses the following important topics:

- The caregiving journey, told through family caregiver stories
- The basics of family caregiving
- Caregiving tips
- Caregiver training
- Caring for yourself

- Legal and financial issues to consider
- Where to turn for help

Caregiver Guide

http://www.nia.nih.gov/Alzheimers/Publications/caregiverguide.htm

Website from the NIA and NIH. Includes links on:

- tips for caregivers
- communication
- bathing
- dressing
- eating
- activities
- exercise
- incontinence
- sleep problems
- wandering
- home safety
- driving
- visiting the doctor
- coping with holidays
- visiting a person with AD
- dealing with the diagnosis
- choosing a nursing home
- hallucinations and delusions

Caregiver Guide — Tips for Caregivers of People with Alzheimer's Disease

http://www.nia.nih.gov/Alzheimers/Publications/CaringAD/

From the National Institute on Aging, a 28-page publication, PDF. Topics for caregivers include:

- Understanding AD
- Caring for a Person with AD

- Understanding How AD Changes People — Challenges and Coping Strategies
- Helping Family Members and Others Understand
- Keeping the Person with AD Safe
- Providing Everyday Care for People with AD
- Adapting Activities for People with AD
- How to Take Care of Yourself
- Getting Help with Caregiving
- Common Medical Problems in People with AD
- Coping with the Last Stages of AD
- End-of-Life Care

Caregiver Resource Directory

http://www.netofcare.org/crd/resource_form.asp

Order a free copy online at the URL shown above, or download a copy (PDF) at: http://www.netofcare.org/content/default.asp#caregiver

"The Caregiver Resource Directory is a practical guide intended to help family caregivers feel less alone and overwhelmed. It offers resources, facts, and advice about caring for a loved one, as well as the caregiver. The Directory is designed as an interactive 3-ring binder with pockets and ample writing space so that caregivers can organize all resource and medical information in one place."

Some of the topics included in the Directory are:

- Tips for new caregivers
- Stress
- Financial and insurance assistance
- Communicating with health care professionals
- Managing symptoms at home
- Handling medical emergencies
- Goals of care
- DNR orders
- Hospice
- Coping with the emotional aspects of caregiving
- Caring for patients with specific illnesses

Caregiver Stress

http://www.4women.gov/FAQ/caregiver.htm

Frequently asked questions—a site from the National Women's Health Information Center of the U.S. Department of HHS. FAQ include:

- What is a caregiver?
- Who are our nation's caregivers?
- What is caregiver stress?
- How can I tell if caregiving is putting too much stress on me?
- What can I do to prevent or relieve stress?
- What is respite care?
- What is the National Family Caregiver Support Program (NFCSP)?
- How can I find out about caregiving resources in my community?
- What kind of caregiver services can I find in my community?
- What kind of home care help is available?
- How will I pay for home health care?
- Who is eligible for Medicare home health care services?
- Will Medicaid help pay for home health care?

Caregiver Support — Open Directory

http://dmoz.org/Health/Senior_Health/Caregiver_Support/

The directory contains an exhaustive list of links.

Caregivers

http://www.hhs.gov/aging/index.shtml

A website from the Department of Health and Human Services. Topics/links include:

- A–Z Topics for Caregivers (healthfinder)
- Caregiving (MedlinePlus—see entry below.)
- Resources for Caregivers (AoA)
- Guide for Caregivers (AoA)
- Support Programs for Caregivers

Caregivers

http://www.nlm.nih.gov/medlineplus/caregivers.html

From the National Library of Medicine, MedlinePlus Health Topics. Articles on caregiving and research on caregiving. An excellent resource for the elderly and their caregivers.

Caregiver's Handbook

http://www.acsu.buffalo.edu/~drstall/hndbk0.html

A 9-part online posting

Caregivers Library

http://www.caregiverslibrary.org/Default.aspx?tabid=1

"The National Caregivers Library is one of the most extensive online libraries for caregivers that exist today. It consists of hundreds of articles, forms, checklists and links to topic-specific external resources." The library is organized into eighteen Caregivers Resources categories, these include:

- Caregiving Basics
- Caring for Yourself
- Care Facilities
- Checklists & Forms
- Disabilities
- Diseases
- Emotional Issues
- End-of-Life Issues
- Glossary
- Government Resources
- Home Care
- Housing Issues
- Legal Matters
- Long-Distance Care
- Medical Care
- Money Matters
- Other Research
- Transportation

Caregiving Overview

http://www.agis.com/Eldercare-Basics/Caregiving-Overview/

An informative page from Assist Guide Information Services (AGIS). Topics/links include:

- Aging in Place
- Assessing Your Situation
- Hiring a Care Manager
- How to Get Help
- Checklists & Assessments
- Listing of Agencies

Caregiving Policy Digest

http://www.caregiver.org/caregiver/jsp/content_node.jsp?nodeid=836

"*Caregiving Policy Digest* is a focused e-newsletter from Family Caregiver Alliance's National Center on Caregiving. The Digest offers a fresh look at the rapidly changing environment of caregiving. Subscribers will receive details on key federal and state legislation, news on innovative public programs, and the latest information on caregiving and long term care policy at national and state levels." Subscribing is free; the link can be found on the website.

CareGuide@Home

http://www.eldercare.com/

"Everything families need to understand, plan, and manage care for their elderly loved one." The site includes a "CareGuide Assessment" designed to help you quickly locate the most relevant resources and information about your elder care situation.

CarePathways

http://www.carepathways.com/mission.cfm

"CarePathways.com was created and is maintained by RNs dedicated to optimizing a family's access to valid information and creditable services about senior care and housing options. It is our goal to educate families about the types of care options available in order to help them to better understand what might be the best choice for their aging loved ones. Access to our on-line databases facilitates the difficult search for home care, assisted living, retirement homes, nursing homes and other long term care facilities."

"Caring for an Aging Loved One"

http://www.pueblo.gsa.gov/cic_text/family/aging/lovedones.htm

"This Life Advice pamphlet about 'Caring for An Aging Loved On' was produced by the MetLife Consumer Education Center and reviewed by the U.S. Administration on Aging of the U.S. Department of Health and Human Services and the National Council on Aging." Topics/links include:

- Introduction
- How Will You Know?
- Developing a Care Plan
- Organizing Documents and Paperwork
- Managing Your Loved One's Affairs
- Providing Home and Community-Based Care
- When Your Loved One Can No Longer Live at Home
- Who Pays for Long-Term Care?
- Taking Care of You
- For More Information

Caring for Older LGBT Families: A Guide for Professionals

http://www.asaging.org/at/at-262/IF_Caring_For_Older_LGBT_Families.cfm

"Only by increasing our awareness of the unique issues facing LGBT caregivers and strengthening our professional competence through ongoing education and training can we become effective change agents, ensuring an LGBT identity no longer automatically places LGBT caregivers at risk of receiving incompetent, ineffective or inappropriate services."

Caring for Someone with Alzheimer's

http://nihseniorhealth.gov/alzheimerscare/toc.html

An NIH SeniorHealth site. Table of contents includes:

- Home Care
- Residential Care
- Safety Issues
- Caregiver Support
- Frequently Asked Questions
- MedlinePlus— more information on Caring for Someone with Alzheimer's

Caring to Help Others

http://www.caringtohelpothers.com/html/index.htm

A online training manual for preparing volunteers to assist caregivers of older adults. A total of approximately 500 downloadable pages. These include an extensive glossary of common caregiving and medical terms.

Caring Today

http://www.caringtoday.com/?gclid=CPS4-vb-0Y0CFRwzYQodJDyTbA

"Practical advice for the family caregiver."

Caring.com

http://www.caring.com/

"Caring.com was created to help you care for your aging parents and other loved ones. Our mission is to give you the information and other resources you need to make better decisions, save time, and feel more supported. Caring.com provides the practical information, easy-to-use tools, and personal support you need during this challenging time. Caring.com features original content focused exclusively on eldercare and end-of-life matters."

Topics/links include:

- health
- housing
- finances
- legal
- life
- daily care

Checklist and Forms for Caregivers

http://www.caregiverslibrary.org/Default.aspx?tabid=70

Topics/links include:

- housing
- money and insurance
- physical and emotional health
- planning and assessment
- record keeping and legal matters
- end of life issues

Children of Aging Parents (CAPS)

http://www.caps4caregivers.org/

A national organization for caregivers. "Children of Aging Parents is a non-profit, charitable organization whose mission is to assist the nation's nearly 44 million caregivers of the elderly or chronically ill with reliable information, referrals and support, and to heighten public awareness that the health of the family caregivers is essential to ensure quality care of the nation's growing elderly population."

DisabilityInfo.gov: Caregivers Resources

http://www.disabilityinfo.gov/digov-public/public/DisplayPage.do?parentFolderId=149

"DisabilityInfo.gov is the federal government's one-stop Web site for people with disabilities, their families, employers, veterans and service members, workforce professionals and many others. A collaborative effort among twenty-two federal agencies, DisabilityInfo.gov connects people with disabilities to the information and resources they need to actively participate in the workforce and in their communities."

Eldercare at Home

http://www.healthinaging.org/public_education/eldercare/

"A Comprehensive Online Guide for Family Caregivers." From the Foundation for Health in Aging. A twenty eight chapter online resource for families and friends who are caring for older people at home. The publication can be ordered online —$19.95.

Eldercare Locator

http://www.eldercare.gov/Eldercare.NET/Public/Home.aspx

Eldercare Locator is a public service of the U.S. Administration on Aging. The Eldercare Locator connects older Americans and their caregivers with sources of information on senior services. The service links those who need assistance with state and local agencies on aging and community-based organizations that serve older adults and their caregivers. There is a three-step process involved in a search, or the user can opt to speak personally to an information specialist at the 800- number listed on the site.

ElderCare Online

http://www.ec-online.net

"The Internet community for elder caregivers. ElderCare Online is a beacon for people caring for aging loved ones. Whether you are caring for a spouse, parent, relative or neighbor, we are committed to providing an online community where supportive peers and professionals help you improve quality of life for yourself and your elder." Eldercare Online provides information for caregivers and many helpful links to resources. There are hyperlinks to a variety of articles, resources, and interactive support groups for caregivers.

ElderCarelink

http://www.eldercarelink.com/about.html

"ElderCarelink is an internet-based referral service—free to consumers—that specializes in eldercare case matching for elders and their families. ElderCarelink assists families in finding a multitude of services, including assisted living, nursing homes, adult day care, private duty nursing, care management and homecare. With participating providers in all 50 states, ElderCarelink identifies qualified eldercare service providers and product suppliers who meet the specific needs for each family's individual situation."

Elderly Caregiver Resources

http://www.way2hope.org/linkmachine/resources/resources_directory_senior_caregiver_support.html

Links to help caregivers of the elderly (not "elderly caregivers" as name of website infers). Caregiver support, help, advice, products and services to help you while you're helping seniors.

"Elderly Caregiving: Choices, Challenges, and Resources for the Family"

http://ucsfhr.ucsf.edu/index.php/assist/article/elderly-caregiving-choices-challenges-and-resources-for-the-family/

A brief but informative discussion of the topic from the University of California, San Francisco.

Family Care Navigator

http://caregiver.org/caregiver/jsp/fcn_content_node.jsp?nodeid=2083

A Family Caregiver Alliance site. "If you are providing care to an older or disabled family member or friend, you know that navigating the long-term care system can be difficult. This state-by-state resource is intended to help you locate government, nonprofit, and private programs in your area. It includes services for family caregivers, as well as resources for older or disabled adults living at home or in a residential facility. It also includes information on government health and disability programs, legal resources, disease-specific organizations and much more."

Family Care Resource Connection

http://www.caregiving.org/fcrc.htm

From the National Alliance for Caregiving. "At the Family Care Resource Connection, family caregivers can search a database of over 1,000 items by topic or key word and find an abstract, a rating and ordering information for each item. The materials are submitted by non-profit organizations, caregiver advocacy groups, disease-specific groups, government agencies and for-profit companies."

Here you will find reviews and ratings of hundreds of books, videos, websites, magazines, fact sheets and other resources addressing the range of issues and questions faced by family caregivers."

A Family Caregiver's Guide to Hospital Discharge Planning.

http://www.caregiving.org/pubs/brochures/familydischargeplanning.pdf

This 20-page booklet includes:

• What Is It?
• Who Does It?

- When Should It Happen?
- What Will Insurance Pay For?
- What Else Should You Know?

Family Caregivers Online

http://www.familycaregiversonline.com/

"An education and information resource for family caregivers of older adults."

Family Caregiving 101

http://www.familycaregiving101.org/

"The National Family Caregivers Association (NFCA) and the National Alliance for Caregiving (NAC)—leaders in the movement to better understand and assist family caregivers—have joined together to recognize, support and advise this vital group of Americans. Family caregivers have been part of America's health care picture for a very long time. Yet, their roles and special needs are just being acknowledged."

"If you're caring for a loved one who is ill or disabled, this site was created for you. It's a great place to find assistance, answers, new ideas and helpful advice—for you and your loved one." Topics include:

- Stages of Caregiving
- How to Manage
- You Are Not Alone
- Find Help

Federal and State Agencies for Seniors

http://www.usa.gov/Topics/Seniors/FederalState.shtml

Official information and services from the U.S. government. Topics/links include federal agencies and state agencies and locators.

FirstGov for Seniors

http://www.usa.gov/Topics/Seniors.shtml

A preeminent site that provides an extensive list of links of interest to senior citizens' and their caregivers, including:

- Caregivers' Resources
    Help providing care, benefits, long-distance caregiving, legal matters, support for caregivers
- Consumer Protection for Seniors
    Consumer fraud, elder rights, advocates for nursing home residents
- Education, Jobs, and Volunteerism for Seniors
    Adult education, AARP working options, Senior Corps
- End-of-Life Issues
    Advance directives, estate planning, hospice
- Federal and State Agencies for Seniors
    Administration on Aging, Social Security Administration, Veterans' Health Administration
- Health for Seniors
    Disease, health care facilities, Medicare, nutrition
- Housing for Seniors
    Reverse mortgages, eldercare, nursing home comparison
- Laws and Regulations Concerning Seniors
    Age Discrimination in Employment Act, Medicare Modernization Act, Social Security Act
- Money and Taxes for Seniors
    Investing, tax counseling, estate planning
- Retirement
    Pension plans, benefits calculator, retirement ages
- Travel and Recreation for Seniors
    Amtrak senior discount, older drivers, travel tips

Frauds Against the Elderly

http://www.amazon.com/Frauds-Against-Elderly-Charles-Sharpe/dp/0786418559/ref=sr_1_6/002-0647889-3028002?ie=UTF8&s=books&qid=1186528693&sr=1-6

This comprehensive and very informative handbook first defines fraud, then discusses why the elderly are targeted, the growing scope of the problem, and why these crimes often go unreported or unsolved. The second section clearly explains 28 of the most common types of fraud — including home improvement scams, health frauds, identity theft and magazine sales — in a manner that allows readers to recognize and avoid the predatory actions of others (whether strangers, friends, or even family members). The third section provides a list of resources and actions to take for those who believe themselves to be the victim of fraud. The book also contains a list of related acronyms, an index and a bibliography.

Full Circle of Care

http://www.fullcirclecare.org/

"We are working together to provide you with support, education, information, and assistance needed to support your efforts to keep your older family members living at home in a secure and loving environment for as long as possible."

Google Directory — Caregivers Resources

http://www.google.com/Top/Health/Senior_Health/Caregiver_Support/

This Google directory has many links for caregivers.

Growing Old in America: Expectation vs. Reality

http://pewsocialtrends.org/assets/pdf/Getting-Old-in-America.pdf

From the Pew Research Center, June 22, 2009. "Getting old isn't nearly as bad as people think it will be. Nor is it quite as good. On aspects of everyday life ranging from mental acuity to physical dexterity to sexual activity to financial security, a new Pew Research Center Social & Demographic Trends survey on aging among a nationally representative sample of 2,969 adults finds a sizable gap between the expectations that young and middle-aged adults have about old age and the actual experiences reported by older Americans themselves." Not directly relevant to the topic of caregiving itself, but a very informative study. Downloadable, 152 pages, PDF.

Guide to Choosing a Nursing Home

http://www.medicare.gov/Publications/Pubs/pdf/02174.pdf

A 68 page online guide from the Centers for Medicare & Medicaid Includes:

- How to find and compare nursing homes in your area
- Your nursing home resident rights
- Where to call for help.
- Tear-out checklist to compare nursing homes

Guide to Long-Term Care (LTC) Insurance

http://www.pueblo.gsa.gov/cic_text/health/ltc/guide.htm or
http://www.pueblo.gsa.gov/cic_text/health/ltc/guide.pdf

From America's Health Insurance Plans (AHIP)—"a national association representing nearly 1,300 members providing health benefits to more than 200 million Americans. AHIP and its predecessor organizations have advocated on behalf of health insurance plans for more than six decades."

Handbook for Long-Distance Caregivers

http://www.caregiver.org/caregiver/jsp/content_node.jsp?nodeid=1034

"An essential guide for families and friends caring for ill or elderly loved ones." Whether you live an hour away or across the country, this booklet offers a roadmap for those new to the challenges of caring from afar for ill or elderly loved ones. Included: how to assess your care situation; develop a care team; hold a family meeting; access community organizations and private agencies; and balance work and caregiving. Free download of the publication, 31 pages, PDF.

Healthy Aging for Older Adults

http://www.cdc.gov/aging/

From the Centers for Disease Control. Topics/links include:

- State of Aging & Health Report
- End-of-Life Issues
- Health Information for Older Adults
- Healthy Brain Initiative
- Links to Organizations
- Publications

Healthy Caregiver

http://www.healthycaregiver.com

A magazine for family and professional caregivers of the elderly.

Help and Resources for Caregivers: Tips for Preventing Caregiver Burnout

http://www.helpguide.org/elder/caring_for_caregivers.htm

Links to topics include:

- What do we need to know as family caregivers?
- Taking care of yourself while caregiving
- Caregiver support groups
- References and resources

iGuard

http://www.iguard.org/

"iGuard is the fastest and easiest way to get personalized, safety alerts and updates about your medicines." A significant new tool on the Web, which promises potentially life-saving help to seniors. This is a free service to access current information about the risk profile of their medications and receive personal drug safety alerts.

Information about Caregiving

http://www.go60.com/caregiving.htm

"Caregiving of older adults covers the fields of independent living, assisted living, home health care, delivery of nutrition and nursing homes. Go60 is dedicated to providing information and resources to assist older adults in extending their lifespan of productive and independent living."

"Keep abreast of developments on the many fronts facing seniors in need of caregiving and their friends and loved ones who take on responsibility. Here you'll find current news and links to timely articles and useful internet resources relating to this rapidly expanding enterprise." News and useful websites for older adults, their friends, and loved ones about assisted living, home health care, and nursing homes.

Lesbian, Gay, Bisexual and Transgender (LGBT) Issues and Family Caregiving (2003)

http://www.caregiver.org/caregiver/jsp/content_node.jsp?nodeid=981

Few subjects in our society fuel debates as heated as those pertaining to sex and sexual orientation. Such debates lead some professionals and heterosexual family caregivers to question whether or not lesbian, gay, bisexual and transgender (LGBT) caregivers need assistance that differs from the assistance needed by the majority community.

This publication from The Family Caregiver Alliance "takes a look at the unique issues facing caregivers who are members of the LGBT community. Includes discussions of obstacles which may prevent LGBT caregivers from fully utilizing available support services, and suggests ways to overcome those obstacles at systems, community and policy levels." Free download, 36 pages, PDF: http://www.caregiver.org/caregiver/jsp/content/pdfs/op_2003_lgbt_issues.pdf.

Mature Market Institute

http://www.metlife.com/mmi/

From MetLife. "Our Mission — the issues of aging and longevity have an ever-changing impact on individuals, families, businesses and society as a whole. We provide objective research and focused thought leadership to render a vibrant portrait of growing older today." Caregiver links on sidebar include: "Since You Care Guides" — up-to-date learning and strategies to help those who care for others, and "Helpful Hints" — step-by-step suggestions for those who need care and their families.

Maturity Health Matters

http://www.fda.gov/cdrh/maturityhealthmatters/index.html

"This online newsletter is about FDA regulated products for older adults, their families, and their caregivers. It focuses on FDA approved products that help people live longer, more productive lives."

Medicare

http://www.medicare.gov/

The official government Medicare site provides many topics for seniors including planning for long-term care, and a nursing home search tool and comparison guide.

National Adult Day Services Association (NADSA)

http://www.nadsa.org/default.asp

"The National Adult Day Services Association (NADSA) is the leading voice of the rapidly growing adult day services (ADS) industry and the national focal point for ADS providers." On the homepage click on the link in the right sidebar: "Find an Adult Day Service."

National Association for Home Care and Hospice

http://www.nahc.org

National Association for Home Care is a Washington, D.C.–based trade organization for home care agencies, hospices, and aid groups. It publishes *How to Choose a Home Care Provider*, which is also available on its website.

National Association of Area Agencies on Aging (N4A)

http://www.n4a.org

"The National Association of Area Agencies on Aging is the umbrella organization for the 655 area agencies on aging (AAAs) and more than 230 Title VI Native American aging programs in the U.S. Through its presence in Washington, D.C., N4A advocates on behalf of the local aging agencies to ensure that needed resources and support services are available to older Americans. The fundamental mission of the AAAs and Title VI programs is to provide services which make it possible for older individuals to remain in their home, thereby preserving their independence and dignity. These agencies coordinate and support a wide range of home- and community-based services, including information and referral, home-delivered and congregate meals, transportation, employment services, senior centers, adult day care and a long term care ombudsman program."

National Association of Professional Geriatric Care Managers (NAPGCM)

http://www.caremanager.org

Geriatric care managers (GCMs) are health care professionals, most often social workers, who help families in dealing with the problems and challenges associated with caring for the elderly. This national organization will refer family caregivers to their state chapters, which in turn can provide the names of GCMs in your area. This information is also available online. Contact NAPGCM for resources, referrals to local Association chapters, and information on counseling and treatment programs.

National Association of State Units/Agencies on Aging (NASUA)

http://www.nasua.org/

"The National Association of State Units on Aging (NASUA) is a non-profit association representing the nation's officially designated state and territorial agencies on aging. The mission of the Association is to advance social, health, and economic policies responsive to the needs of a diverse aging population and to enhance the capacity of its membership to promote the rights, dignity and independence of, and expand opportunities and resources for, current and future generations of older persons, adults with disabilities and their families."

National Caregivers Library

http://www.caregiverslibrary.org/

"The National Caregivers Library is one of the most extensive online libraries for caregivers that exists today. It consists of hundreds of articles, forms, checklists and links to topic-specific external resources."

National Center on Senior Transportation (NCST)

http://seniortransportation.easterseals.com/site/PageServer?pagename= NCST2_home page

"Mission: To increase transportation options for older adults and enhance their ability to live more independently within their communities throughout the United States."

"Goals: To achieve the mission through the development, collection and distribution of information and resources for use by communities, transportation providers, state and local governments, aging and human service providers, and older adults and their caregivers. Technical assistance, research toward solutions, strategic communications and building partnerships among stakeholders are additional functions of the center." Click on the link in the left sidebar "For Older Adults & Caregivers." The resources listed offer directories of transportation-related services, information about safe driving, and policy discussions.

National Clearinghouse for Long-Term Care Information

http://www.longtermcare.gov/LTC/Main_Site/index.aspx

This web site was developed by the U.S. Department of Health and Human Services to provide information and resources to help you and your family plan for future long-term care needs.

National Family Care Support Program (NFCSP)

http://www.aoa.gov/AoARoot/AoA_Programs/HCLTC/Caregiver/index.aspx

"The National Family Caregiver Support Program, established in 2000, provides grants to States and Territories, based on their share of the population aged 70 and over, to fund a range of supports that assist family and informal caregivers to care for their loved ones at home for as long as possible." Click on "Resources and Useful Links."

National Institute on Aging (NIA)

http://www.nia.nih.gov

"NIA, one of the 27 Institutes and Centers of NIH, leads a broad scientific effort to understand the nature of aging and to extend the healthy, active years of life. NIA's mission is to improve the health and well-being of older Americans through research, and specifically, to: support and conduct high-quality research on: aging processes, age-related diseases, special problems and needs of the aged."

National Respite Locator

http://www.respitelocator.org

"The National Respite Locator Service helps parents, caregivers, and professionals find respite services in their state and local area to match their specific needs."

NIA Publications Catalog

http://www.niapublications.org/pubs/englishpuborder.asp

The National Institute on Aging has a wealth of information available. Most of these materials are FREE. An online order form can be used to send in orders by fax or mail. The publications are grouped into the following areas:

- general information
- "Age Pages"
- "Fact Sheets"
- caregiving resources
- information for health professionals
- information in Spanish

Older Gays Involved in Caregiving for Family Members at Rates Equal to or Exceeding Those in the General Population

http://www.thetaskforce.org/press/releases/pr694_061704

"Nearly half of lesbian, gay, bisexual and transgender (LGBT) individuals over 50 are heavily involved in caregiving, both for members of the families they grew up in and for same-sex partners and close friends, according to a new study released today by the National Gay and Lesbian Task Force Policy Institute, Pride Senior Network, and the Fordham University Graduate School of Social Service. In fact, gay people over 50 may actually be caregivers at a higher rate than their counterparts in the general population."

Practical Skills Training for Family Caregivers (2003)

http://www.caregiver.org/caregiver/jsp/content/pdfs/op_2003_skills_training.pdf

"An overview of the day-to-day, hands-on strategies and skills caregivers need to maintain a frail older or chronically ill individual at home." This publication from The Family Caregiver Alliance is available as a downloadable PDF document, 23 pages.

Publications for Caregivers

http://www.caregiving.org/pubs/brochures.htm

A National Alliance for Caregiving (NAC) webpage. "Being a caregiver is challenging, but even more so if you're not equipped with quality information. On this page you can download copies of Alliance publications that provide information on where to find help and how to make sure your loved one is getting the best possible care." Click on the links to download these publications.

Resource Directory for Older People

http://www.nia.nih.gov/HealthInformation/ResourceDirectory.htm

"The 120 page *Resource Directory for Older People* is intended to serve a wide audience including older people and their families, health and legal professionals, social service providers, librarians, researchers, and others with an interest in the field of aging. The directory contains names, addresses, phone numbers, and fax numbers of organizations which provide information and other resources on matters relating to the needs of older persons. Inclusion in the directory does not imply an endorsement or recommendation by NIA or AoA."

Resources for Caregivers

http://www.cchs.net/health/health-info/docs/2600/2690.asp?index=9955

A listing of links from the Cleveland Clinic Health System — includes national organizations and government resources.

The Ribbon — Care for Caregivers

http://www.theribbon.com/index.asp

"The Ribbon Online, a website inspired by *The Ribbon Newsletter*, created to provide information for caregivers dealing with Alzheimer's and Dementia."

Senior Citizens' Resources

http://www.seniors.gov

Information on consumer protection, education and training. Links include retirement planner, seniors and computers, services, strategic planning, tax assistance, travel and leisure, and work and volunteering. There are also links to federal portals, federal agencies, and state websites.

Seniorlink

http://www.seniorlink.com/

"Seniorlink is dedicated to helping seniors age with dignity and independence. Explore our site to learn more about all of Seniorlink's eldercare solutions." Topics include

- families
- employers
- care managers
- caregivers

ShirleyBOARD

http://www.shirleyboard.com

"Where caregivers network." ShirleyBOARD is a free online community with tools and features to help those caring for aging loved ones stay organized and communicate with one another. The site allows caregivers to centrally store important information, keep a log of daily activities for family and friends to view, and network with other caregivers for support and inspiration.

The Three Stages of Caregiving

http://www.strengthforcaring.com/manual/about-you-am-i-a-caregiver/the-three-stages-of-caregiving/

"Here is some insight to help you understand the different caregiving stages, and tips and resources you might find useful as you adapt to your new or evolving role." The stages:

1. Early: Surprise, Fear, Denial, Confusion, Sadness (What is happening to my loved one?)
2. Middle: Frustration, Guilt, Resentment, Conflicting Demands (How long does this last?)
3. Late: Sadness, Guilt, Surrender, Regrets, Relief, Solace, Closure (How do I respect the needs of my loved one?)

Today's Caregiver

http://www.caregiver.com

Weekly newsletter on caregiving. "Helping caregivers cope with the demands of caregiving, whether it's caring for an aging parent, a disabled loved one, or a patient coping with a difficult disease." Includes discussion forums and extensive links to specific information resources.

United Way — AIRS 211 Program

http://www.211.org

"Every hour of every day, someone in the United States needs essential services — from finding an after-school program to securing adequate care for a child or an aging parent. Faced with a dramatic increase in the number of agencies and help-lines, people often don't know where to turn. In many cases, people end up going without these necessary services because they do not know where to start. 2-1-1 helps people find and give help." A site from United Way of America (UWA) and the Alliance for Information and Referral Systems (AIRS).

U.S. Senate Special Committee on Aging

http://aging.senate.gov/resources.cfm

Links to topics include:

- General Aging Links
- Health Care for Seniors
- Long Term Care
- Elder Fraud and Abuse
- Social Security and Retirement Savings
- Older Workers
- Emergency Preparedness for Seniors
- Assisting Seniors with Rising Energy Costs
- Affordable Senior Housing

Vital Records: Where to Obtain

http://www.cdc.gov/nchs/w2w.htm

The links on this federal government site are provided for those users who want direct access to individual state and territory information. To use this valuable tool, you must first determine the state or area where the birth, death, marriage, or divorce occurred, then click on that state or area. Please follow the provided guidelines to ensure an accurate response to your request. Note: the federal government does not distribute certificates, files, or indexes with identifying information for vital records.

Web Site Links (NCOA)

http://www.healthyagingprograms.com/content.asp?sectionid=76

From the National Council on Aging. Two categories of links: Health Information, and Organizations. Many links in each category.

The Well Spouse Association

http://www.wellspouse.org/

"This site gives support to husbands, wives and partners of the chronically ill and/or disabled. They provide a bi-monthly newsletter, *Mainstay*, mutual aid support groups in many areas; letter writing support groups; an annual conference; and other regional and weekend meetings around the country. The organization also works to make health care professionals and the general public aware of the difficulties caregivers face every day."

Widowhood & Living Alone

http://www.seniors-site.com/widowm/index.html

"Information on living alone and widowhood by and for senior citizens"—and for caregivers of this population of the elderly. Topics include:

- Widowhood—coping with the loss, the funeral arrangement, business matters, and suggestions.
- Women Going It Alone—income, employment, housing, health health-care costs, women as caregivers, safety and security, and divorce.
- Men Living Alone—health concerns and issues that place older men at risk.
- Living Solo—What you can do to make living alone rewarding.
- Loneliness—dealing with the feelings.

Your Aging Parent.com

http://www.youragingparent.com/

"This site is designed for adult children caring for an aging parent but most of the material also applies if you're helping your spouse, or assisting a child or sibling with special needs, or a friend or family member."

Appendix A

Because We Care: A Guide for People Who Care

Author's note: This publication was prepared by the Administration on Aging, U.S. Department of Health and Human Services in 2003. It is no longer available from the AoA, but can be downloaded and printed from a number of sites on the Internet. The publication is in the public domain.

INTRODUCTION

If the last century is any indication, we are headed for exciting times in the decades ahead. There will be new technologies to make our every day lives easier. We can expect breakthroughs in medical research that will astonish us and give millions more hope for healthy, longer lives. And, if there are as many advances in international and community relations, hopefully we will also see a more inclusive embrace of humankind.

All of these developments will be good news for the nation's millions of family caregivers. Assistive devices are already saving many caregivers from placing their own health and well-being at risk, but there are many day-to-day activities that remain difficult to complete without some kind of assistance. There also are diseases like Alzheimer's, Parkinson's, cardiovascular disease, and diabetes for which cures or preventive measures are desperately needed. Here is where the kindness and love of family, friends, and neighbors have made the difference for so many older persons and their caregivers.

We, at the Administration on Aging, have met and talked with hundreds of family caregivers from across these United States. Their experiences have left an indelible impression in our hearts and minds. What they have shared with us, about the extraordinary gifts of love they are giving older relatives and friends in need of care, inspired us to offer *Because We Care: A Guide for People Who Care*.

So many family caregivers have said that they wish they had known more about how to provide care, about the resources that exist, about how to get help for their loved ones and themselves, about what they can do to be sure that their own quality of life is optimal. So many family caregivers have said that future caregivers need to have the opportunity to understand caregiving and its dimensions ahead of time, in order to be prepared for the challenges that may arise. So many persons receiving care have said that they are concerned about the health and well-being of their caregivers.

To each and every one of you who is or may be a member of the community of caregivers, we dedicate this guide. We respect and acknowledge your love and your dedication. The guide is yours to use. We hope that it will be of help ... because we care.

PREFACE

Because We Care: A Guide for People Who Care is being offered by the U.S. Administration on Aging (AoA) as a resource guide to the growing number of Americans who are caring for an older family member, adult child with disabilities, or older friend. This *Guide* provides information and a range of suggestions to make caregiving easier and more successful — whether you are the caregiver or the person who ensures that your family member or friend receives the best possible care from others.

Because We Care recognizes the wealth of information which can be accessed by caregivers via the World Wide Web. It organizes the information to address particular aspects of caregiving. To access web-based information, just click on the text words or phrases that are highlighted. Where information is not yet available at other web sites, we fill the gap and provide you with information.

We have listed web sites that offer a range of information that caregivers can use. However, references from this AoA web site or from any information services sponsored by the AoA to any non-governmental entity, product, service or information does not constitute an endorsement or recommendation by the Administration on Aging or any of its employees.

The AoA is not responsible for the contents of any of the "off-site" web pages referenced. While the *Because We Care* Guide includes links to sites that may reference other information, the Administration on Aging does not endorse ANY specific products or services mentioned. Full responsibility for any use of these links rests with the user.

FOREWORD

Because We Care: A Guide for People Who Care is being offered because fully one-fourth of American families are caring for an older family member, an adult child with disabilities, or a friend. This guide offers you a range of suggestions to make caregiving easier and more successful, whether you are a caregiver or the person who ensures that your loved one receives the best possible care from others. Caregiving takes time, effort, and work. It can challenge you intellectually and emotionally, teach you flexibility and strengthen your problem solving abilities. Over time some care receivers recover and/or improve. If so, this can be very satisfying, but even when those being cared for are not able to improve, your efforts are enhancing the life of someone you care so much about, someone you love.

I. WHERE CAN WE TURN FOR HELP?

Introduction

Caregiving may be one of the most important roles you will undertake in your lifetime. Typically it is not an easy role, nor is it one for which most of us are prepared. Like most people, you may have questions about your care receiver's chronic illness or disability. If you have a job and are juggling several responsibilities or if your family member or friend needs a lot of assistance, you may need help with caregiving, too. Whether you are expecting to become a caregiver or have been thrust into the role overnight, it is useful to know where you can get information and help.

Individuals Who Can Help You Find Assistance

There are information services with staff who can help you figure out whether and what kinds of assistance you and your care receiver may need. You can call:

- The National Eldercare Locator, a free service funded by the Administration on Aging (AoA), for information about assistance that is available in communities across the nation.
- Your State Agency on Aging for information and assistance. Look in your phone book under "aging" or "senior services."
- Your local Area Agency on Aging (AAA) for information and assistance right in your community. Look in your phone book under "aging" or "senior services."

Generally, state and area agency on aging services are funded with federal, state, and other monies. These government-funded services are often targeted to those most in need. While there are no income criteria for many services, sometimes, you may have more service options, if you can pay for private help. You can contact your State or Area Agency on Aging for information and assistance.

There are several services that can help you plan for the care that will be needed. They can be accessed through the state or area agency:

- Care management services: a care manager can assess your relative's needs and resources and draw up a plan to help her remain as healthy and independent as possible.
- Social work services: hospitals and nursing homes usually have social workers and discharge planners.
- Attorneys, who specialize in such areas as wills, trusts, and probate, and financial planners can help with the legal and financial aspects of caregiving.

Supportive services for the person needing care can include:

- Transportation
- Meals
- Personal care
- Homemaker

(See the section on "What Services Can Help Us?" for information on supportive services.)

Other types of resources for caregivers are:

- Caregiver support groups
- Caregiver organizations

- Organizations like the Alzheimer's Association
- Chat rooms on caregiving on the Internet
- Family members and friends who have been caregivers

And don't forget, if you are an employee covered under the federal Family and Medical Leave Act 14, you are entitled to take up to 12 weeks of unpaid leave during any one year to care for an older relative.

II. WHAT SERVICES CAN HELP US?

Introduction

If you are a caregiver and need help, chances are that assistance is available in your community. There are many different government and privately funded services that may be available. Most of the programs and services mentioned in this guide are federally funded through the Older Americans Act. You can get information about these services and programs in communities throughout the nation by contacting the Eldercare Locator.

While some services are free, others are fee-based. In-home and community-based services that you might find helpful include:

- Personal and in-home services
- Home health care
- Transportation
- Meals programs
- Cleaning and yard work services
- Home modification
- Senior centers
- Respite services including adult day care

Personal and In-Home Care Services

Personal and in-home care assistants help with bathing, dressing, preparing meals, house cleaning, laundry, toileting, and other personal "activities of daily living."

Home Health Care

Home health care includes such care activities as changing wound dressings, checking vital signs, cleaning catheters and providing tube feedings. Home health care staff also may provide some personal care services and light housekeeping. If the older person for whom you are caring is recuperating from an accident, operation, or illness, he or she may be able to receive home health care assistance through a *Medicare* certified home care agency. If older persons cannot care for themselves because of physical functioning, health problems, or because they no longer are able to mentally process things, they may be eligible for skilled nursing care or physical, speech, or occupational therapy. In these cases, home health care also may be available. Ask your older relative's doctor if your family member is eligible for these services.

To find out more about home health care, check "Home Health," a publication by the Centers for Medicare and Medicaid Services (CMS)—formerly the Health Care Financing Administration (HCFA)—the federal agency that administers the Medicare program, or talk to the doctor who is caring for your family member. Medicare usually pays for home health care services for two or three hours a day, several days a week, and for the medical care provided by a doctor, nurse, or other health professional. Such care tends to be for a limited time.

If the person for whom you are caring has a limited income and assets, he or she may be able to receive home health care, personal care, or hospice services as well as occupational, physical, or speech therapy through Medicaid (a federal-state program, administered by CMS at the federal level). Some older persons with limited assets and income are eligible for help through both the Medicare and the Medicaid programs. If this is the case, your care receiver may be able to obtain personal and/or home health care services on a long-term basis instead of being cared for in an extended care facility. Otherwise, in-home and community-based services may be available through an Area Agency on Aging.

Middle and higher-income persons often pay out-of-pocket for *personal and home health care services.* If you hire staff through a home care agency, ask the agency how they screen their staff and if staff is bonded. Agencies charge you for the costs of doing business; i.e., for management, administration, and recruiting workers. This can be quite expensive, but there are ways to make help more affordable. For example, you can explore the possibility of directly hiring a personal or home health care assistant. If you choose to hire help, be sure to check their qualifications and references carefully. Remember, you will then be an employer, and you may need to cover Social Security and other benefits. (See the Section on How Do I Hire a Home Care Employee?)

Respite Care

Respite care can be a voluntary or paid service. It can be provided in your relative's home, in an extended care facility, such as a nursing home, or at a senior center or adult day care center. Respite care can extend for a few hours or for several weeks. It provides the caregiver with opportunities to take care of personal affairs, to get some rest, or to take a vacation.

Transportation

Transportation services are vitally important to older persons with limited mobility. Transportation enables them to go to their doctors, to the pharmacy, and to attend to day-to-day activities.

Many public mass transit systems are fitting buses and other vehicles with hydraulic lifts and other aids to assist older persons and others that have physical disabilities. Sometimes several transit systems operate independently of each other. Transportation options may be available through private companies and private non-profit organizations. These include public fixed-route, demand-response, ride sharing, volunteer drivers, limousines, buses, vans, and regular and special purpose taxis. Some services provide an escort to assist older people.

To arrange transportation for an older person in your community, contact your local Area Agency on Aging (it is listed under "aging," "elderly," or "senior services" in the government section of your telephone directory). Area Agencies on Aging provide older persons and their caregivers with specific information and assistance in getting transportation and other supportive services in the community. If you want information about safe driving and older drivers you may want to contact the National Highway Traffic Safety Administration.

Meals

Good nutrition can help to improve health and control a range of conditions and diseases. The National Elderly Nutrition Program, funded by the Administration on Aging, provides meals to older persons in need and their spouses. Older persons who participate in the group meal program have an opportunity to socialize, receive nutrition education, and take part in other activities, including health screenings.

Elderly persons who are ill or frail may be able to receive a government-subsidized home-delivered meal. To find out about home-delivered meals programs and other meals programs, please contact the National Eldercare Locator or your State or Area Agency on Aging.

If these meals are not available, see if your grocery store prepares food orders for pick-up or if it provides home-delivery service. A growing number of grocery and meal services are available via the Internet including some that offer organic, ethnic and kosher foods. Many local restaurants deliver meals without additional charge and some even offer senior discounts on meals. A growing number of restaurants offer special low-fat and low-salt meals.

There also are local and national franchised meals delivery services. These are listed in the yellow pages of the telephone directory under "foods—take out"; some can be found on the Internet.

Cleaning and Yard Work Services

An Area Agency on Aging may be able arrange for chore and yard maintenance services or put you in touch with religious, scout or other volunteer groups that provide one-time or occasional services to older persons who need help. Of course, you can hire a cleaning service or yard maintenance firm, but this may be more expensive than hiring someone that works as an independent contractor.

Home Modification, Improvement, and Weatherization Programs

Home modification and repair programs can make homes safer and more energy efficient. They can result in greater independence for an older person with disabilities. The Home Modification Action Project at the University of Southern California's Andrus Gerontology Center has online consumer oriented information and publications on accommodations and modifications and how to pay for these. There is information on how to make dwelling units safe for persons with Alzheimer's Disease. There also is information for builders, a library of useful publications on housing adaptation, and links to other useful web sites.

Senior Centers

Seniors Centers offer older people a safe environment where they can take part in a range of activities led by trained personnel that promote healthy lifestyles and where they can develop a network of friends.

Meal and nutrition programs, information and assistance, health and wellness programs, recreational and arts programs, transportation services, volunteer opportunities, educational opportunities, employee assistance, intergenerational programs, social and community action opportunities and other special services are often available through a senior center.

Adult Day Care Services

For older persons with serious limitations in their mobility, those who are frail, and those who have medical and cognitive problems, adult day care centers can provide care in a safe, structured environment. Adult day care can provide relief to working caregivers and respite for full-time caregivers. Adult day care services include personal and nursing care, congregate meals, therapeutic exercises, and social and recreational activities.

Most adult day care centers, like senior centers, are supported through public and non-profit organizations. Fees may range from a few dollars a day to close to $200, depending on the services needed. The National Council on the Aging maintains a directory of adult day care centers and links to other related sites.

III. HOW CAN I CARE FOR BOTH OF US?

Introduction

Sometimes we are so deeply concerned about the well-being of the person for whom we are caring, that we forget our own needs. We "burn the candle at both ends" and become exhausted, emotionally stressed or ill, compromising our own quality of life and our ability to care for our family member.

Some Caregiver Do's and Don'ts

We owe it to ourselves and to our families to also maintain our own physical and emotional health by:

- Getting sufficient sleep
- Eating a healthy diet
- Exercising and staying physically fit
- Choosing appropriate health care professionals and having periodic health checkups
- Not abusing alcohol and drugs
- Spending social time with family and friends
- Pursuing our own interests
- Seeking support from family, friends, professionals, or your religious advisor or joining peer support groups
- Using appropriate in-home and community-based services.

Keep in mind that it is normal to feel angry, frustrated, or depressed from time to time. Caregiving can be a difficult as well as a rewarding undertaking. If you are feeling stressed, angry, or depressed:

- Remove yourself from the situation by walking away, even if it's just around the house
- Talk to someone with whom you feel close
- Call a hot line
- Talk with your doctor or other health professional
- Write down your feelings in a journal

If you find that you frequently are angry or depressed or that your emotions are getting out of control, you may benefit from counseling, and/or get relief in the form of respite, caregiver support groups, and supportive in-home services.

IV. HOW CAN I IMPROVE OUR QUALITY OF LIFE?

Introduction

Older Americans and their caregivers sometimes fall victim to myths that become self-fulfilling prophecies. One is that being old means being sick. The other is that old age and dementia go hand in hand. The truth, however, is far more positive.

Truth # 1. Old age and sickness are not synonymous. The majority of older people are healthy, and, if they are not, many chronic conditions and illnesses can be controlled or corrected.

Truth # 2. While the incidence of dementia does increase as people age, the majority of older people score well on tests of mental functioning. Those who do not often have underlying medical problems that account for decreases in mental functioning.

Maximizing Your Care Receiver's Independence and Health

Keeping or restoring health in the later years often requires more effort and determination than when we are younger. It includes:

- A healthy diet. If your relative or friend has medical problems, you can ask the physician if changes in diet should be made and whether you should consult a registered dietician for additional information.

  Supplements of certain vitamins and minerals, if advised by the physician or dietician. Always remember that more is not always better, that nothing takes the place of a healthy diet, and that some vitamins and herbs can be dangerous, if taken in excess or in the presence of certain medical conditions.

- Exercise. If your older relative or friend is reasonably healthy, he or she can begin a regular program of exercise including stretching, weight training, and low impact aerobics, after discussing it with his or her physician.

  Exercise can help to avoid accidents, improve strength and mobility, lower blood pressure, and help to prevent or control some diseases. If your care receiver is frail or ill, you can ask the physician about what exercises may be appropriate. Your older relative or friend may want to begin such an exercise program under a physical therapist's supervision. The physical therapist can show you how to do range of motion, stretching, and strengthening exercises. Over time, these exercises can help to increase strength and mobility.

- Monitoring, in consultation with your relative's primary care physician and pharmacist, both over the counter drugs and prescription medications to ensure that there are no adverse drug reactions or bad reactions between several drugs. Make sure that all medications are appropriate for your care receiver's individual needs and that the rules for safely taking drugs are being followed.

- Staying involved with family and friends.

- Taking part in community activities, such as going to senior center activities.

- Keeping an active mind with activities ranging from reading to card and board games as well as using a computer.

- Learning about assistive devices that can enhance your older relative or friend's independence and safety.

- Ensuring home safety with such modifications as ramps and low thresholds, better lighting, and nonskid rugs to enhance your care receiver's safety and independence.

Choosing Health Care Providers

It is important for your older relative or friend to have a primary care physician, usually an internist, family medicine practitioner or geriatrician, as well as, specialists if needed. When choosing physicians, check their qualifications. What is their academic background and experience? Are they board certified in their practice area? You may want to accompany your older relative or friend to the appointment and take notes. This helps to insure that you both understand what medical course of action is recommended and gives you the opportunity to observe the interaction between the doctor and your relative.

The health care provider's attitude toward older persons is important. Is he or she interested in caring for older persons, and willing to take the extra time to conduct a thorough examination, to ask questions, and let you and your relative ask questions?

One note of caution — if your relative is not in managed care, try to choose health care providers that are either preferred or participating providers, if your insurance requires it to make standard payments. Otherwise, you may be responsible for a large percentage of the bill. This is also true for hospitals and all of their subcontractors, such as anesthesiologists.

If your care receiver is limited in his or her physical abilities, ask the physician about the possibility of having physical, speech, or occupational therapy. You also should ask about assistive devices that are available.

V. WHAT HOUSING OPTIONS ARE AVAILABLE?

Introduction

There are many times when it is not possible for a caregiver and care receiver to live together.

The level of care that your spouse, relative or friend needs may require highly skilled health care personnel on a regular basis. In this case, an extended care facility, such as assisted living or a nursing home, may be a better care alternative.

Your relative or friend may live in another town and does not want to move. There may not be room in your home, or family members, including your relative, may not want to live together.

Whatever the reasons, living in different housing does not mean that you cannot be a good caregiver. You and your relative will, however, need to make arrangements for additional help and/or services as needed — either in his or her present home or in a new housing arrangement.

Points to Consider When Choosing Housing and Living Arrangements

When providing services to older persons who have limitations in their mobility and multiple needs, the type of housing and living arrangements you choose become critical keys in assuring that they get the care they need. Housing and care in this instance go hand in hand. There are many types of housing arrangements available for older persons, and they often overlap in the types of care and services they provide.

Before making a housing choice, you and your older relative should assess present needs and envision, as best as possible, how these needs may change in the future.

- What options will be open to you if the need for more supportive housing and living arrangements arises?
- Will your family member need to move to another care arrangement?
- Are these facilities available in the community, and how much will they cost?
- How are you going to pay for housing and services now and in the future?
- If you enter into housing that requires a substantial deposit at the time of admission, will some of the money be returned if your relative decides to leave?
- What guarantees do you have that the facility is financially secure?

You and your older relative will want to ask these questions before making a decision about moving into a new housing arrangement. If this arrangement involves a large entrance fee or deposit or the signing of a contract, you also will want to consult a lawyer before making the commitment.

Guidelines for Choosing Housing Options

Regardless of what the facility is called, check it out thoroughly before making a decision. The types of facilities listed below range from informal home-share arrangements to commercial enterprises, government-sponsored facilities, and housing options administered by nonprofit organizations. Some are licensed or accredited, others are not.

- Accreditation is an evaluation of a facility's operation against a set of standards. The Continuing Care Accreditation Commission — a membership organization of continuing care communities— is one such organization.
- Licensing is an evaluation of a facility's operation in accordance with government regulations. About half of the states currently regulate assisted living facilities.
- Many skilled and intermediate care nursing facilities are accredited to accept patients under the Medicare and/or Medicaid programs, which means that they must meet certain standards and provide certain services.

Regardless of these considerations, you are responsible, in large part, for ensuring that the facility is the right one for your spouse, relative or friend.

Even if you are not thinking about housing options in the foreseeable future, it is wise to have several in mind in case an emergency arises and you need temporarily care for your relative. Home care agencies often do not have staff available to fill in on short notice, and you may need the services of a long-term care facility.

You can:

- Start your preliminary search by phone.
- Visit those facilities that have the services your care receiver wants and needs.
- Take your older relative to see the facility. Better yet, visit several and let your relative make the final choice, if at all possible.

If your relative is able to make sound decisions, and does not like any of the housing options or does not want to move into a facility after visiting several, keep looking or further explore the possibility of home care in her home or yours. Use a check list (this check list can be used as a general guide for all types of housing) to ensure that the housing arrangement is the right one for your relative.

Types of Housing and Living Arrangements

Listed below are types of housing and living arrangements, what they generally offer, and for whom they are intended. Added to these considerations are those of costs. While some housing options are modestly priced, others, especially those that are for-profit, tend to be expensive. You can go to the section entitled "How Can We Afford Long Term Care?" for information about government assistance programs for housing and care.

- Retirement communities are planned towns with a range of housing, services, and care options.

- Continuing care communities offer varying levels of care in the same building or on the same campus. When Selecting a Continuing Care Retirement Community or retirement community, remember they may encompass everything from housing for independent living to assisted living and skilled nursing home care. Therefore it may be difficult to identify what is offered simply because a facility has a certain name. These communities are usually designed for older persons with substantial financial resources.

- ECHO Housing is a self-contained housing unit temporarily placed on a relative's lot that is suitable for older persons who are largely self-sufficient.

- Accessory Apartments are self-contained apartments in the care receiver's home, your home or the home of another caregiver. Designed for older persons who may be largely self-sufficient or need help with housekeeping, cooking, and personal care—commonly referred to as activities of daily living (ADLs).

- Shared Housing can be in the home of the older person or in someone else's home. Common areas, such as kitchens and dining rooms, are shared. This type of housing offers the older homeowner added income or the older renter an inexpensive place to live. It may offer companionship, and the possibility of having someone else around, at least part of the time, to help out with chores or in case of emergencies, but this depends on the persons sharing the house. This type of arrangement can work well for those elderly who are independent, but who would welcome a little extra income and/or help. It is important, however, to check the person's references carefully before making a decision.

- Congregate Senior Housing usually offers small apartments. Some offer group meals and social activities. They are designed for persons who are largely independent and do not need personal care or help with activities of daily living.

- Adult Foster Care is usually provided in private homes—often by the owner of the residence. The home usually provides meals, housekeeping and sometimes personal care and assistance with ADLs.

- Senior Group Homes are located in residential neighborhoods and offer meals, housekeeping, and usually some personal care and assistance with Activities of Daily Living (ADLs). Usually a caregiver is on site, with medical personnel making periodic visits.

Both adult foster care and group homes may be referred to as Board and Care Homes or Residential Care Facilities.

Assisted Living may provide everything, including skilled nursing care. Others provide only personal care, assistance with ADLs and/or social activities. These may also be called Retirement Homes or Residential Care facilities to name a few.

Nursing Homes provide an array of services including 24-hour skilled medical care for total care patients; custodial care; therapy for patients convalescing from hospitalizations; and personal care and help with activities of daily living for persons with dementia, chronic health, and/or mobility problems.

VI. WHEN YOUR CARE RECEIVER LIVES WITH YOU

Introduction

American society is often a muddle of contradictions, and this is certainly true when it comes to families. On the one hand, we cherish the concept of the extended family and laud the ideal of multiple generation households. On the other we cherish our privacy and fiercely defend our independence. It is thus important for you, your relative or friend, and other family members to weigh the pros and cons of living together. This is especially true if you are working or have other family responsibilities. You will need to consider these before you enter into an arrangement that may or may not be the best option for you and your care receiver.

Pros and Cons

It is probably best for everyone involved to discuss what you imagine the pros and cons of living together to be. Every family's situation is unique. Listed below are some of the benefits and drawbacks that may result. It is important for your relative or friend to take part in the decision, and to be a valued and contributing member of the family with meaningful roles, whenever possible.

On the plus side:

1. If your care receiver needs considerable care, you will save the expense of a long-term care facility or, at least, some in-home services.
2. You know that your care receiver is getting the best possible care because you are either providing it yourself or directly overseeing the care.
3. You will be able to make major decisions that can give you a sense of empowerment.
4. You will have more time to spend with your family member or friend.
5. Your children will have an opportunity to spend more time with their grandparent(s) or other older relative, have an important lesson in compassion and responsibility, learn about their roots, and develop a sense of family continuity.
6. If your care receiver is fairly healthy, he or she may help with household tasks, and/or with the children.

On the other side:

1. You may have less time for yourself and/or other family members and if you work you may find conflicts between your job and caregiving responsibilities. Some employment versus care giving responsibilities may be relieved, especially in light of the technology revolution that is taking place, where telecommuting may now be an option.
2. Depending on your lifelong relationship, you may find that you and/or your relative resent changes in your relationship that may take place.
3. You will lose at least some of your privacy.
4. Other family members may resent the new arrangement.
5. There may be less space for everyone in the family.
6. You may find that hands-on caregiving is too physically and/or emotionally demanding.

If you decide that you do want to live together, you might want to try it on a trial basis, if possible. You might consider renting or subletting your care receiver's home on a short-term basis so that he or she has the option of returning home if the new arrangement does not work out to everyone's satisfaction.

You will want to consider what, if any, physical changes need to be made to your residence and how much they will cost.

Will Intergenerational Living Work in Your Home?

As a guide, you may want to ask the following questions:

1. Is your home large enough so that everyone can have privacy when they want it?

2. Is there a separate bedroom and bath for your family member, or can you create an accessory apartment?

3. Are these rooms on the first floor? If not, can your relative climb stairs safely?

4. Can you add to or remodel your home to provide a first-floor bedroom and bath?

5. Do you need to add safety features such as ramps and better lighting?

6. Does the bathroom have a shower, is it large enough to accommodate a wheelchair, if needed, and can safety features, such as grab bars, be installed to prevent falls?

7. Are door openings wide enough for a wheel chair?

You also may want to set some ground rules for privacy.

Sharing Time Together

Obviously, if you want your care receiver to live with you, you will want to share times together.

1. Set aside times to talk.

2. Involve your care receiver, if possible, in family outings and social events.

3. Invite other family and friends to your home, and let them know that you are available to come to their house as well. All of them will not respond, but some will.

4. Even errands, such as shopping, can be something of a social event, and give your relative a chance to participate in decision-making.

At the same time, you want to ensure that other members of the family do not feel that they have been "displaced" and that they are as important to you as ever.

VII. LIVING DAY TO DAY

Introduction

As caregivers, we sometimes become so involved in the day-to-day efforts to keep things going that we tend to forget that each day can be an opportunity to try new approaches and activities that will make a positive difference in our life and the life of those we care for.

Some things that can bring about positive changes for the better include:

- Standing back and taking a look at your situation — what is working well and what isn't — and finding ways to make changes for the better
- Establishing routines that effectively meet your care receiver's needs
- Improving your physical surroundings
- Physical, speech and occupational therapy and/or exercise
- Assistive devices, which range from special eating utensils to specially equipped telephones, that increase independence and safety
- Improved nutrition
- Carefully monitoring medications and their interactions
- Intellectual stimulation
- Social interaction
- Spiritual renewal
- Employing home and/or health care personnel who demonstrate that they really do care and who will work to foster independence
- Finding ways to economize on your work load
- Filling each day with activities to which you can both look forward

Hands-On Caregiving

If your older relative or friend needs considerable help, a well-planned routine can make the more demanding parts of your caregiving day go more smoothly, take less time and help to ensure that your care receiver does not develop problems which could be prevented.

- Make a list of all the things you need for morning and bedtime routines, buy several of these items, and have them close at hand, such as bathing items, medications, and clothing. This saves time and keeps you from having to search or leave the room for them when you are helping your older family member. If you use items in several different places, have duplicate items stored in these rooms, such as the bathroom and bedroom.

- If possible, have someone help you with the morning and bedtime routines, if your older relative needs a lot of assistance, since getting up and going to bed often are the most challenging times of the day.

- Practice good oral hygiene that includes tooth-brushing, denture cleaning, and cleaning around the gums, preferably after every meal. Good oral hygiene helps to prevent tooth decay, tooth loss and gum diseases, as well as secondary infections that can result from poor dental care. Persons with disabilities or medical problems may need special care in addition to daily hygiene routines.

- If your older family member is disabled, has poor eyesight or cognitive impairments, you may need to remind them about personal hygiene and/or assist them. If your care receiver is incontinent, it is especially important to ensure that he or she is clean at all times, to use protective (barrier) creams, and to change incontinence aids and clothing as often as needed.

    Poor hygiene can result in diaper rash and blistering of the skin. Poor hygiene also can contribute to the development of decubitus ulcers (pressure sores) and other problems that cause pain, discomfort and serious, even life threatening infections. In older women, tight fitting clothing and diapers can lead to yeast infections.

There are new commercial products that make incontinence much less of a problem than it once was because they keep clothes and bed linens clean and dry. You also can discuss ways in which your care receiver's incontinence may be corrected with your health care provider, including exercises and surgical procedures.

Older persons with limited movement should be turned in bed on a regular basis to prevent pressure sores. Correct bedding, such as sheepskin or egg carton bed coverings and/or an air mattress, helps to prevent pressure sores. It is important to move older persons with disabilities at least once an hour, even if it just to reposition them, to do range of motion exercises, and to have them sit in various chairs that offer sufficient support.

Make lists of:

- Morning and bed time routines

- Medical personnel with their area of expertise, addresses and telephone numbers

- Home health agencies
- Other people who can help or fill in, if you need additional help
- Lawyers and financial advisors
- Where needed items are kept, such as thermometers and blood pressure monitors
- Medications, when they are to be taken, and where they are stored
- Exercise schedules and directions
- Emergency contacts in addition to 911

These lists and other needed information can be put into a clearly marked notebook and kept where others can easily find them in your older relative's room. This book should be complete enough so that someone filling in for you will know exactly what is needed and what to do.

Tips on Safety

Quick, easy, and readily available ways to communicate with others that can help in an emergency are a must for you and your older family member or friend. You can get:

- A cordless speaker phone with memory so that you can simply hit one button in an emergency and get help without compromising the safety of your care receiver.
- A cellular phone, if you and your care receiver travel.
- A signal system which will summon help with the push of a button, if you leave your care receiver alone, at times.
- A specially equipped telephone with speed dialing, a large digital display for easy reading, and ring and voice enhancer, if your care receiver has hearing problems.
- An intercom, that will alert you if your care receiver is having problems when you are in another room.
- Smoke detectors on each floor, which should be periodically checked to ensure that they are operating properly.

If your family member is disabled, you will want to ensure that he or she:

- Has a clear path through each room, that there are no rugs or raised room dividers to trip over, and no slippery floors. You can carpet the bathroom with all weather carpeting to help prevent falls. This can be pulled up in sections, if it is wet.

117

- Uses a cane or walker, if needed.
- Is secure in his or her wheel chair. If your older relative is weak a tray that attaches to the wheel chair can prevent falls and gives your care receiver a place for drinks, magazines, etc. It is important to ensure that the wheels are securely locked when doing transfers, or if the older person's chair is on an incline.
- Cannot fall out of bed. If the bed does not have guardrails, you can place the wheel chair or other guards next to the bed, and position your older relative in the middle of the bed so that she or he can turn over without fear of falling.

Meals

As people age, they sometimes experience problems with chewing and swallowing, but there are ways to minimize these problems. The need for certain nutrients in older person's diets may also change.

Avoid foods that are high in:

- Saturated fats
- Salts, chemical preservatives and additives
- Sugar and calories that do not enhance nutrition, but may add to excessive weight gain.

There are numerous ways to obtain pre-prepared and easy to prepare meals that are nutritious time savers.

For older people who are homebound, meal times can be pleasant social events, when you can be together and talk. If your relative or friend is confined to bed, you can sit and talk while he or she eats and bring a tray in for yourself. There are a host of eating utensils and accessories that make eating easier for persons with disabilities.

Caring for Your Home

- Use an attractive plastic tablecloth or place mats that are easy to clean and an attractive towel, apron or other covering for your care receiver's clothes, if there is a tendency to spill food. Be sure that it is large and long enough to cover their laps and fold it inward before taking it off to avoid spillage on the floor. Consider having a vase of flowers (even if they are artificial) on the table or next to the bed, if your older relative is confined to bed, and open the curtains and let the sun shine in.

- Use lightweight, plastic easy-grip glasses, or cups with handles. If there is a lot of spillage, try a drink holder with a lid and plastic straw insert.
- If clothes are wrinkled, you can put them in the dryer with a wet towel or sponge on a warm setting. This often saves a lot of time ironing.
- If your care receiver is incontinent, you can:
  1. Use washable or disposable pads on the bed above the sheet
  2. Rubberized sheets underneath the bed sheet.
  3. A stain and water resistant mattress pad.
- If the mattress does become soiled, it will need to be thoroughly cleaned and aired after being sprayed with a safe (always read the label) anti-bacterial cleaning agent. You can ask your doctor or pharmacist for recommendations.
- You can use water-resistant pads or heavy towels on the wheelchair or furniture that your care receiver uses. If you travel, keep pads in the car for use on the car seat and when visiting other places.
- When buying towel sets, you may want to purchase extra wash cloths since these are used more frequently and wear out faster. Thermal blankets also are useful because they are warm, lightweight, and easy to wash.

Exercise

In consultation with your care receiver's physician and physical therapist, you can plan a routine of exercises. Exercises even for bed and wheelchair-bound older persons help to improve:

- Circulation
- Lung and heart function
- Posture
- Mental alertness

Help to prevent:

> Diabetes
> Pressure sores
> Osteoporosis
> Heart disease
> Stroke

If appropriate, encourage your relative to do a little more physical activity each week. Vary the exercises and challenge them to do better. Exercise with them. If they are confined to a bed or wheelchair, try to get them to exercise at least five minutes every hour, and again, regularly change their position to prevent pressure sores.

Clothing

Regardless of our age or physical condition, we want to look and feel our best. Today's clothing options make that a much easier goal to reach. When buying clothing, consider the following:

- Clothing that is washable and wrinkle-free saves on dry cleaning bills and ironing time.
- Slacks and skirts that have elasticized waistbands or tie waistbands are easier to get on and off and are more comfortable.
- Clothing with snaps or zippers and some that button down the front are easier to manipulate.
- Shoes that will not slip off easily, and have a non-skid tread.
- Interchangeable and color-coordinated clothing. e.g. slacks and tops that can go with several others.

Entertainment, Entertaining and Travel

Boredom can sap our intellect and spirit, but you can change this by creating activities that you and your care receiver look forward to and by sharing these with others. There are many activities that frail and disabled older people can enjoy.

You can:

- Check the TV listings and choose your favorite programs to watch each day rather than having the TV going nonstop.
- Get large print and talking books from the library and read together.
- Play card and board games— they stimulate mental activity.
- Check for special events that are low-cost or free. Invite a friend or family member to join you, preferably one who can drive or help you if your care receiver has a physical disability.
- Go out to lunch or the early-bird specials at restaurants.
- Visit an art-hobby store and see what is available in the way of arts or crafts projects that you and your care receiver can enjoy.
- Invite family or friends over for dinner or lunch. If you have limited funds to entertain or do not have time to prepare food have them over for

dessert or snacks, ask each of them to bring something, or to chip in on a carryout meal.

- Plan day trips to local places of interest. Again invite a friend or family member to join you.

- If you can afford to do so, go on a vacation. You can share the adventure and expense with other family members or friends. Many places offer senior discounts. Make sure that they can accommodate your needs, especially if your care receiver is disabled. Large hotel and motel chains now go out of their way to help, if you make your needs known to them. In addition, there are companies and organizations that plan trips for persons with limitations in their mobility. Many travel books have special sections on accommodations, travel, and activities for those with limited mobility.

- If you have the room, invite friends or family members to come and stay with you for a while in your home.

- Check colleges, religious organizations, and community centers for free courses and other activities.

- Visit museums, galleries, botanical and zoological parks or a petting zoo.

- If appropriate, get a pet. Your local shelter or humane society has many nice pets available for adoption.

- Get a computer with Internet access so that you can e-mail friends, join in chat rooms, learn about things that are of interest to you, and enjoy computer games.

- Ask your local Area Agency on Aging about friendly visitor, volunteer, and telephone reassurance programs.

- Many fraternal, religious, and social organizations have activities specifically for older people. This can be a great way to extend your circle of friends and supportive network.

VIII. HOW CAN WE AFFORD LONG-TERM CARE?

Introduction

Some older persons have very limited incomes and assets and are eligible to participate in a number of benefit and assistance programs. Others have adequate assets to cover their regular living expenses, but cannot pay for long-term care for a long time.

Programs for Older Persons with Limited Incomes and Assets

MEALS AND IN-HOME SERVICES

If the person for whom you are caring has limited income and resources, there are programs that can help. You may want to find out about the Food Stamp program that provides coupons for purchasing food. Your older relative or friend may be able to participate in a group or home-delivered meals program and receive supportive in-home services through an Area Agency on Aging. These options are discussed in the section on What Services Can Help Us?

BENEFIT PROGRAMS

In addition to the Old Age and Survivors Benefit program, commonly called Social Security, the Supplemental Security Income program provides benefits to persons with limited incomes and assets who are blind, disabled, or 65 or older. To find out about these programs, contact your Area Agency on Aging or the Department of Social Services where your older relative lives. If your older relative served in the armed forces during wartime or has a service-connected disability, you should inquire about Veterans benefits and services.

HOUSING PROGRAMS

There are housing programs for older persons with limited incomes who do not own their own homes. These programs include public housing and Section 8 rental certificates that are available to low-income persons regardless of age and Section 202155 housing for older persons. These are programs of the Federal Department of Housing and Urban Development, but you can contact your local housing authority for information about these rental-housing options in your older relative's community.

There also are a number of U.S. Department of Agriculture Rural Housing Service programs for persons living in rural areas. These range from loans to buy homes to home-improvement and rent subsidy programs.

HEALTH BENEFITS

Finally, you may want to check out the federal Centers for Medicare and Medicaid Services programs, such as the Qualified Medicare Beneficiary program, that assist low-income Medicare beneficiaries. These programs help low-income seniors pay all or part of the premiums for Medicare. For additional information about Medicare and Medigap policies click on Medicare and You. The Medicaid program covers many of the medical expenses not covered by Medicare, such as prescription medications, and, in some cases, long-term home health and in-home personal care. Each state sets its own income and asset eligibility requirements for Medicaid benefits.

Most states now have programs that pay family caregivers to provide homemaker, chore, and personal care services. Most use state funds to compensate families, while other states use Medicaid waiver funds. Contact your Area Agency on Aging or your department of social services for more information.

You also may want to explore the possibility of purchasing Medigap and/or long-term care insurance. Medigap insurance is private insurance that usually covers the cost of health care not covered by Medicare as well as Medicare deductibles. Long-term care insurance generally pays a set amount or a percentage of costs for long-term care both at home and in long-term care facilities. However, long-term care insurance may:

- Be quite expensive for persons aged 70 or older.
- Unavailable to persons of advanced ages.
- Not pay in the case of preexisting conditions.

Most experts recommend buying long-term care insurance when you are in your fifties and in reasonably good health.

TAX DEDUCTIONS AND CREDITS

Some out-of-pocket expenses associated with long-term care, including transportation to medical appointments, long-term care insurance premiums, prescription drugs, privately hired in-home health care employees, and changes to a dwelling or car for medical reasons, are tax deductible as medical expenses. The expenses must be for the care of a chronically ill individual who needs help with at least two activities of daily living or requires "substantial supervision to protect against threats to health and safety due to severe cognitive impairment." Tax credits generally benefit low-income taxpayers. Tax credits usually require the caregiver to live with the care recipient and to be employed outside the home.

COVERING LONG-TERM CARE COSTS

Many caregivers and care receivers cannot qualify for public-funded assistance because they have substantial income and assets but do not have the financial resources to pay for needed services for extended periods of time without impoverishing themselves. In caregiving, many families deplete the resources they accumulated over a lifetime. If this happens, caregivers may try to provide all of the needed care. This can be difficult for spouses who are frail or have medical problems, as well as for family members especially those who work and/or have children. In these instances, you and your older relative should consider asking other family members to contribute to the cost of care and/or to provide some of the care on a regular basis.

If formal part-time care and informal help from families is insufficient, the older person can enter a skilled nursing or other long-term care facility that is certified to accept Medicaid patients. In some communities, however, facilities have waiting lists of persons who want to enter as Medicaid patients.

Ways to Maximize Your Assets

Most caregivers need to budget wisely and maximize their relative's assets. There are several ways to do this:

- If your older relative wants to remain at home, she could live on one floor and rent out rooms in the rest of the house through a house-sharing arrangement. This arrangement can bring in a substantial amount of income where housing is relatively expensive or in short supply.

- Another option is to rent out her residence, and have her move to a smaller home, an apartment, your residence, or other housing option. Renting out a residence and house sharing both provide income that will usually keep pace with inflation and offer tax advantages. Improvements, repairs, and all or part of the house can be depreciated. If your older relative lives in the house, she also can claim some of the utilities as a tax exemption.

- If the house is in an unsafe area, or in a neighborhood or community that is declining in value, it may be best to sell. A federal tax exemption may available for a person 55 or older who sells his or her home.

- Another possibility is to provide room and board to someone in exchange for caregiving and/or other needed services. There are several drawbacks to this arrangement, however. It may be difficult to:
  - Prove to the IRS that your older family member has received home health services in exchange for room and board.
  - Depreciate the room for tax purposes.
  - Ensure that the home care employee honors his or her part of the arrangement — providing services in exchange for room and board.

The better arrangement is to rent out the room(s) and pay a home care worker. Some home care workers work as independent contractors (check to see if they have a federal tax ID number to work as an independent contractor). While this arrangement frees you from dealing with social security, workers compensation, unemployment taxes, and other withholding taxes— all of which can be complex and time-consuming, there are Internal Revenue Service definitions that govern whether a person is considered to be a contractor or an employee. Thus, be sure to consult an income tax preparer, lawyer, or financial planner before considering this arrangement. If the home care worker is truly an independent contractor then he or she is responsible for paying social security and other taxes.

Contact your insurance company to be sure you are covered against possible liability should property be stolen, damaged, or destroyed, or if a renter or home care employee suffers injury. If you pay the home care worker as an employee, there are companies, listed in the yellow pages under payroll preparation services, which issue salary checks and arrange for withholdings for a fairly nominal fee. Reverse Equity Mortgages are another option if an older person wants to remain at home and receive monthly payments from a lending institution. The upfront costs for negotiating this type of loan can be considerable, however. Before making a decision, talk to your lawyer and, if possible, a home equity conversion counselor.

Sale-lease back arrangements allow older people to sell their homes and remain as lifetime tenants. However, this arrangement is legally complex, can impact on an older person's eligibility for Medicaid and similar benefits, and precludes benefiting from any future gains in the value of the property.

Other ways to save money include:

- Checking to see if there is property tax relief for older home owners and what the eligibility requirements are.
- Joining clubs or organizations that offer group supplemental health and car insurance plans and discounts on other items and services.
- Buying at discount and thrift stores, during sales and with coupons.
- Checking with mass transit and taxi companies about senior discounts, nonpeak hour ride discounts, and free ride services for persons with low incomes.
- Asking plumbers, trash pick-up services, restaurants etc. if they offer discounts to older customers— many do, but sometimes only if you ask.

You may be able to save 10 to 75 percent on some items and services, if you follow these suggestions.

Lastly and probably most importantly, be sure your relative's assets and your assets are carefully reviewed, if you are helping with expenses. Are you getting the best return on your investments without risking your principle? Are you aware of all of your older relatives' bank accounts, stocks, bonds or other assets? What about pension plans? Some older persons are not getting the money to which they are entitled from pension plans. Having reviewed your assets, what changes can you make to bring in more income? Read good investment books, talk to your bank, your lawyer, and/or find a qualified investment planner or advisor for some ideas.

IX. HOW DO I HIRE A HOME CARE EMPLOYEE?

Introduction

Today, [2003] one in four American families cares for an older relative, friend, or neighbor. An estimated 25 to 40 percent of women care for both their older relatives and their children. Half of all caregivers also work outside the home. It is no wonder then that caregivers often need help. Depending on your work, living, and family arrangements, there are a number of things you can do to make caregiving easier.

Ways to Make Caregiving Easier

Work Options and On-the-Job Training Programs. If you are a working caregiver, it is important to discuss your needs with your employer. Tele-commuting, flextime, job sharing or rearranging your schedule can help to minimize stress. Increasingly, companies are offering resource materials, counseling, and training programs to help caregivers.

Involving Older Children. Older children living at home may be able to assist you and/or your older family member. Such responsibility, provided it is not overly burdensome, can help young people become more empathic, responsible, and self-confident and give you needed support.

Asking Other Family Members to Help. You can and should ask other family members to share in caregiving. A family conference can help sort out everyone's tasks and schedules. Friends and neighbors also may be willing to provide transportation, respite care, and help with shopping, household chores or repairs.

Determining the Type of Care You Need

If you decide to hire a home care employee, you need to determine how much and what type of help your older relative needs. Following are descriptions of some of the types of home care personnel:

- Housekeepers or Chore Workers may be supervised by the person hiring them and perform basic household tasks and light cleaning. Chore Workers often do heavier types of cleaning such as washing widows and other heavy cleaning.
- A Homemaker may be supervised by an agency or you and provides meal preparation, household management, personal care, and medication reminders.
- Home Health Aides, Certified Nurse Assistants, or Nurses Aides, often referred to as home health care workers, are supervised by a home care agency's registered nurse and provides personal care, help with bathing, transfers, walking, and exercise; household services that are essential to health care; and assistance with medications. They report changes in the patient's condition to the RN or therapist, and complete appropriate records.

Sometimes, home care employees take on several of the roles described above.

General Eligibility Requirements for Home Care Benefits

Medicare may pay for home health care services through a certified home health care agency, if a physician orders these services. Home health care agencies focus on the medical aspects of care and provide trained health care personnel, including nurses and physical therapists. For a patient to be eligible for services paid for under Medicare, she must need skilled nursing assistance, or physical, speech, and/or occupational therapy. Home health care workers are a supplement to this care and usually help the older person for three hours a day, several days a week.

If your older family member or friend needs additional hours of care or requires custodial care, she may be eligible for services under Medicaid. The state where she resides determines if her income and assets qualify her for Medicaid covered services. Otherwise, you or your older relative must cover the cost of having a home care worker.

Home care agencies, which can be nonprofit or for-profit, recruit, train, and pay the worker. You pay the agency. Social Service agencies, in addition to home care services, may provide an assessment of the client's needs by a nurse or social worker, and help with the coordination of the care plan. If services are being covered under Medicare, your doctor, care manager, or discharge planner will probably make arrangements for a home health care agency.

Selecting an Agency

If you select an agency, ask the following questions. Those questions starred with an asterisk should also be asked, if you are hiring the home care employee.

- What type of employee screening is done?
- Who supervises the employee?
- What types of general and specialized training have the employees received?*
- Who do you call if the employee does not come?
- What are the fees and what do they cover?*
- Is there a sliding fee scale?
- What are the minimum and maximum hours of service?*
- Are there limitations in terms of tasks performed or times of the day when services are furnished?*

Unless your older friend or relative needs care for a limited number of hours each day, the rates charged by home care agencies for homemaker, home health aide services and van services for transportation are often beyond the means of middle income families. If this is the case, you may want to explore the option of hiring a home care employee directly.

Hiring a Home Care Employee

Avenues for hiring home care aides include:

- Asking other caregivers for referrals
- Going to senior or other employment services

- Contacting agencies that assist displaced homemakers and others entering the job market
- Advertising in the newspapers

Screen home care employees carefully to ensure that they have the necessary qualifications, training, and temperament.

Interviewing Applicants

Your interview with a prospective home care employee should include a full discussion of the client's needs and limitations, with a written copy of the job description; the home care worker's experience in caregiving and his or her expectations.

Special Points to Consider

- If the older person needs to be transferred from a wheelchair, make sure that the aide knows how to do this safely. If the aide does not know how to bathe a person in bed or transfer, but is otherwise qualified, it may be possible to provide the necessary training, but make sure she can do it before hiring her.
- Do not try to hire someone on a 7-day-a-week basis. No employee can remain a good employee for long, if she does not have time for her personal needs and interests. Additionally, aides who live in or sleep over cannot be expected to be on call 24 hours a day. If your older relative needs frequent help or supervision during the night, you should hire a second home care aide, or have a family member fill in.
- If your older relative needs a considerable amount of help, live-in help may be available, which can be less expensive than hourly or per day employees. However, keep in mind that you will be providing food and lodging and that it may be more difficult to dismiss live-in aides, especially if they do not have alternative housing available. It also is important to ensure that the aide has her own living quarters, and that she has some free time during the day, sufficient time to sleep, and days off.

References

Have applicants fill out an employment form that includes their:

- Full name
- Address

- Phone number
- Date of birth
- Social Security number
- Educational background
- Work history
- References

Ask to see applicants' licenses and certificates, if applicable, and personal identification including their Social Security card, driver's license, or photo ID. Thoroughly check their references. Ask for the names, addresses, phone numbers, and dates of employment for previous employers, and be certain to contact them. If there are substantial time gaps in their employer references, it could indicate that they have worked for people who were not satisfied with their performance. Talk directly to former employers rather than accepting letters of recommendation.

With the applicant's permission, it is also possible to conduct a criminal background check.

Job Expectations

When hiring a home care aide, it is important to list the job tasks and to ask applicants to check those they are willing to perform. You should also discuss:

- Vacations
- Holidays
- Absences
- Lateness
- Benefits and wages
- The amount of notification time each of you should give if the employment is terminated or if she resigns.

If you work and are heavily dependent on the home care assistant, emphasize the importance of being informed as soon as possible if she is going to be late or absent so that you can make alternative arrangements. It is helpful to keep a list of home care agencies, other home care workers, neighbors, or family members who can provide respite care, if needed.

Be clear about:

- The employee's salary.
- When he or she will be paid.
- Reimbursement for money the aide may spend out of pocket.

Needed Information

When hiring a home care assistant, if at all possible spend a day or two with him or her, so that you can go through the daily routine together. If this is not possible, have another home care aide, a relative, or friend remain with the new employee at least during the first day. Also, you will need to inform the home care worker, both verbally and in writing, about the older person's:

- Likes and dislikes.
- Special diets and restrictions.
- Problems with mobility.
- Illnesses and signs of an emergency.
- Possible behavior problems and how best to deal with them.
- Therapeutic exercises.
- Medications—where they are located, when and how they are taken, and how to reorder them.
- Dentures, eyeglasses, and any prosthesis.

Also provide information, verbally and in writing, about:

- How you can be contacted.
- Contacts in case of an emergency.
- Security precautions and keys.
- Clothing.
- Medical supplies, where they are kept, and how they are used.
- Food, cooking utensils, and serving items.
- Washing and cleaning supplies and how they are used.
- Light bulbs, flashlights and the location of the fuse box.
- The location and use of household appliances.

Transportation

If free or low-cost transportation is not available, try to hire someone who drives since this saves you substantial amounts of money in taxi or commercial van ride fares. If the home care employee is going to drive your family car, you must inform your insurance company, and provide a copy of the aide's driver's license to your insurance agent. Your insurance company will check to see if the license has been revoked, suspended, or if the aide has an unsatisfactory driving history. If the home care assistant has a car, discuss use of her car on the job and insurance coverage.

Insurance and Payroll

Check with your insurance company about coverage for a home care employee, and contact the appropriate state and federal agencies concerning Social Security taxes, state and federal withholding taxes, unemployment insurance, and workman's compensation.

If you do not want to deal with these somewhat complicated withholdings from the employee's salary, payroll preparation services can issue the employee's check with the necessary withholdings for a fee.

Some home care aides work as contractors. Even in these cases, you must report their earnings to the Internal Revenue Service. Before employing an aide on a contract basis, consult your financial advisor or tax preparer to make certain that you are following the IRS rules that govern contract workers, since there can be a fine line between who is considered to be an employee versus a contractor. (For additional information about contractors and employees go to the section on "How Can We Afford Long-Term Care?)

Ensuring Security

Regardless of who cares for your elderly relative, protect your private papers and valuables by putting them in a locked file cabinet, safe deposit box, or safe. Make arrangements to have someone you trust pick up the mail, or have it sent to a post box where you can pick it up.

Check the phone bill for unauthorized calls, and, if necessary, have a block placed on 900 numbers, collect calls, three way calls, and long-distance calls. You can always use a prepaid contacting card for long distance calls or arrange for a pin number for your personal use from your telephone company.

Protect checkbooks and credit cards. Never make them available to anyone you do not thoroughly trust.

Review bank, credit card statements, and other bills at least once a month, and periodically request credit reports from a credit report company. Your bank can provide you with the names and addresses of these companies.

If you do leave valuable possessions in the house, it is best to put locks on cabinets and closets and to have an inventory with photographs.

Protecting Against, Identifying, and Handling Abuse

Although abusive situations are not common, you must be alert to the possibility. They are one of the primary reasons why it is so important to carefully check the references of a prospective home care aide. You can help to prevent abuse situations by:

- Ensuring that the home care assistant thoroughly understands what the position entails, your care receiver's medical problems and limitations, as well as behavior that could lead to stressful situations.
- Ensuring that the home care aide is not overburdened.
- Keeping the lines of communication fully open so that you can deal with potential problems.

Following are possible signs of abuse or neglect:

- Personality changes in your older relative or friend.
- Whimpering, crying, or refusing to talk.
- Unexplained or repeated bruises, fractures, burns, or pressure sores.
- Weight loss.
- An unkempt appearance.
- Poor personal hygiene.
- Dirty or disorganized living quarters.
- Confusion, excessive sleeping, or other signs of inappropriate sedation.

If you suspect that an abusive situation exists, don't wait for it to be tragically confirmed. Find a way to check either by talking to the older person in a safe situation or, if necessary, by installing monitoring devices. If you witness, or are told by a reliable source, about neglect; physical abuse; emotional abuse, including yelling, threatening, or overly controlling, possessive behavior, which often involves isolating the older person from others; seek help, if necessary, and replace the home care aide as quickly as possible. If the situation appears serious, remove your care receiver from the premises and place him or her with another family member or in a facility that offers respite care. Always ensure that your relative is safe before confronting or dismissing the worker, especially if you are concerned about possible retaliation.

Once you have ensured your relative's safety, report the aide to Adult Protective Services so they can take appropriate actions to prevent the aide from gaining employment with other vulnerable elders. If the abuse is of a serious nature including, serious neglect, physical injury, sexual abuse, or the misuse of the funds of the older person, you should also contact the police.

Supervising a Home Care Worker

Once you have hired a home care worker, make sure that the lines of communication are fully open and that both you and the worker have a clear understanding of the job responsibilities to the older person and to each other. Explain what you want done and how you would like it done, keeping in mind that the home care employee is there to care for the older person and not the rest of the family.

If the home care worker lives in, try to ensure that he or she has living quarters that provide you, the older person and the assistant the maximum amount of privacy possible.

Once the home care aide is on the job, periodic and/or ad hoc meetings can be held to discuss any problems the home care assistant or the older person may have with the arrangement and to find ways to resolve them. It is important to be positive and open in your approach to resolving difficulties. In most cases, they can be corrected.

However, if, after repeated attempts, you find that major problems are not resolved satisfactorily it may be best to terminate the relationship, and seek another home care employee. During this time, it may be necessary for your older relative to reside temporarily in a long-term care facility or for you to hire an aide through an agency. It is best to have reserve funds on hand should such an emergency arise. While home care may not be less expensive than nursing home care or assisted living, it offers older people the opportunity to remain at home. What is more, it affords a degree of flexibility and choice for the at-risk elderly that few other living arrangements can provide.

X. LIVING WITH ALZHEIMER'S DISEASE

Introduction

Caring for someone with Alzheimer's disease or other forms of dementia can be very difficult. Alzheimer's disease is a progressive, degenerative disease of the brain. It is the most common form of dementia. Profound changes in personality and mental functioning are not unusual. Often, our relationships are changed significantly by this.

Signs of Dementia

Signs of dementia can vary from one person to another. Frequently they include:

- Increasing levels of forgetfulness
- An inability to carry out simple tasks

- Difficulty in remembering words or in forming coherent sentences
- Confusion, hallucinations, or paranoia

If dementia is suspected, consult a physician familiar with Alzheimer's disease as soon as possible. Sometimes medications, underlying illness such as strokes, depression, or other conditions, mimic dementia. When this is the case, problems can be corrected, improved, or controlled.

Dealing with Alzheimer's Disease

Alzheimer's disease is not reversible. However, early diagnosis is important because the progression of the disease can often be slowed with the help of medications and the symptoms also can be managed. Early detection means time for everyone to plan ahead.

Most caregivers want to know what to expect, how to deal with changes that result from Alzheimer's, help that might be needed, and how to find it. Persons with Alzheimer's disease and their caregivers can find help through the Alzheimer's Association and the Alzheimer's Disease Education and Referral Center. These organizations provide excellent information to caregivers of persons with Alzheimer's disease.

XII. WHO WILL CARE IF I AM NOT THERE?

Introduction

As caregivers, we cannot assume that we always will be able to provide care. Even if we are able to be active caregivers, it is important to establish both emergency and long-term alternative care plans for our older relative or friend, and to make sure that the necessary legal documents are in place.

Legal Documents and Care Plans
That Should Be in Place

Every adult should have at least a power of attorney, a living will or medical directive and a will or trust in place so that his or her wishes can be followed. If your older family member does not have these legal directives, you both should consult an attorney and have the appropriate documents drawn up.

When making alternative long-term care arrangements, you will want to discuss the matter with your care receiver(s), if at all possible, and follow their wishes about the person(s) or facility that would care for them, if you were unable to do so. If your care receiver(s) want to live with another family member or friend, you will, of course, want to discuss this arrangement with the proposed caregiver to ensure that it is agreeable.

If your relative can make informed choices about an alternate caregiver, living arrangement, and other matters, it will be easier to make long-term plans, if you have a power of attorney. If your older relative or friend cannot make informed choices it may be necessary to seek appointment as a conservator and/or guardian. This requires an appointment from the court to act on your care receiver's behalf regarding matters of care and financial dealings. Whenever possible, discuss your plans for alternative living arrangements or caregiver choice with your older family member or friend and with other close family members as well as the designated caregiver. This will help to avoid opposition in the future that could lead to serious problems.

If you are the only possible informal caregiver, you and/or your relative can appoint a trusted friend or perhaps a committee composed of several friends to oversee your relative's care, or you may decide that it is best to have a lawyer act as your care receiver's representative. These arrangements also should be legally established.

Once you have decided on an alternate caregiver(s), it will be necessary to ensure that they, too, have the legal power needed to make decisions, should your care receiver be unable to do so. This may involve a durable power of attorney, a special medical power of attorney, and, in some states, a special power of attorney, if property is to be bought or sold, or a guardianship and/or conservatorship. As stated before, you should ensure that both you and your care receiver have medical directives, living wills and estate wills and/or trusts established, if there are financial resources available for your care receiver. In choosing a long-term care housing arrangement it is a good idea to select one that can provide varying levels of care so that your care receiver will not be forced to move, if his or her medical condition changes.

Short-term emergencies don't require the same amount of legal planning, but they must be considered. If you are unable to look after your care receiver, you will need to make arrangements with:

- a relative or friend
- a facility that provides short-term respite care (many nursing homes and assisted living facilities offer such care)
- a home care agency
- a geriatric care manager.

Remember that home care agencies often cannot provide services on short notice, and that you may need to have more than one family member or friend as a backup person. For information on sources of assistance in choosing care alternatives see the section on Where Can We Turn for Help? For information on housing alternatives and living arrangements see the section on What Housing Options Are Available?

Appendix B

So Far Away:
Twenty Questions for
Long-Distance Caregivers

This appendix was adapted from *So Far Away: Twenty Questions for Long-Distance Caregivers* a publication which was Developed by the National Institute on Aging (NIA), part of the National Institutes of Health. It is now in the pubic domain. The unabridged publication can be downloaded from http://www.nia. nih.gov/healthinformation/publications/longdistancecaregiving/, 48 pages, PDF.

This booklet focuses on some of the issues unique to long-distance caregiving, and is a gateway to ideas and resources that can help make long-distance caregiving more manageable and satisfying. It often refers to caregiving for aging parents but, in fact, it offers tips you can use no matter whom you are caring for, be it an older relative, family friend, or neighbor. There's also a resource list at the end that can help you find more information.

THE 20 QUESTIONS

1. What Is Long-Distance Caregiving?

Long-distance caregiving takes many forms—from helping manage the money to arranging for in-home care; from providing respite care for a primary caregiver to helping a parent move to a new home or facility. Many long-distance caregivers act as information coordinators, helping aging parents understand the confusing maze of home health aides, insurance benefits, and durable medical equipment.

Caregiving is often a long-term task. What may start out as an occasional social phone call to share family news can eventually turn into regular phone calls about managing health insurance claims, getting medical information, and arranging for respite services. What begins as a monthly trip to check on Mom may turn into a larger project to move her to a nursing facility close to your home.

If you are a long-distance caregiver, you are not alone. Approximately 7 million adults are long-distance caregivers, mostly caring for aging parents who live an hour or more away. Historically, caregivers have been primarily mid-life, working women who have other family responsibilities. That's changing. More and more men are becoming caregivers; in fact, men now represent over 40 percent of caregivers. Clearly, anyone, anywhere can be a long-distance caregiver. Gender, income, age, social status, employment — none of these prevent you from taking on caregiving responsibilities.

CAREGIVER BASICS—WHAT YOU SHOULD DO (OR THINK ABOUT DOING)

1. Seek out help from people in the community: the next door neighbor, an old friend, the doctor. Call them. Tell them what is going on. Make sure they know how to reach you.

2. Take steps to identify options to help the primary caregiver. He or she may not need the help now, but having plans and arrangements in place can make things easier if there is a crisis.

3. Try to find a directory of senior resources and services by checking with a library or senior center for lists of resources. Get several copies— one for yourself and one for the primary caregiver. This helps everyone learn what's out there and perhaps to start "plugging into the networks." Don't forget to check for updates.

4. Pull together a list of prescriptions and over-the-counter medications. Get doses and schedules. This information is essential in a medical emergency. Update it regularly.

5. When you visit, go through the house looking for possible hazards (such as loose rugs, poor lighting, unsafe clutter) and safety concerns (such as grab bars needed in the bathroom). Stay for a weekend or week and help make needed improvements.

6. Find out if your parent has an advance directive stating his or her health care treatment preferences. If not, talk about setting one up. If so, make sure you have a copy and you know where a copy is kept. You might

want to make sure the primary caregiver has a copy. The doctor should also have a copy for the medical record.

2. How Will I Know If Help Is Needed

In some cases, the sudden start of a severe illness will make it clear that help is needed. In other cases, your relative may ask for help. When you live far away, you have to think carefully about possible signs that support or help is needed. You might want to use holiday trips home to take stock.

Some questions to answer during your visit include:

- Are the stairs manageable or is a ramp needed?
- Are there any tripping hazards at exterior entrances or inside the house (throw rugs, for instance)?
- If a walker or wheelchair is needed, can the house be modified?
- Is there food in the fridge? Are there staple foods in the cupboards?
- Are bills being paid? Is mail piling up?
- Is the house clean?
- If your parents are still driving, can you assess their road skills?
- How is their health? Are they taking several medications?
- If so, are they able to manage their medications?
- What about mood: Does either parent seem depressed or anxious?

3. What Can I Really Do from Far Away?

Many long-distance caregivers provide emotional support and occasional respite to a primary caregiver who is in the home. Long-distance caregivers can play a part in arranging for professional caregivers, hiring home health and nursing aides, or locating assisted living and nursing home care. Some long-distance caregivers help a parent pay for care, while others step in to manage finances.

Caregiving is not easy for anyone, not for the caregiver and not for the care recipient. From a distance, it may be especially hard to feel that what you are doing is enough, or that what you are doing is important. It usually is.

Free Information Available from NIA

NIA has many free publications including the popular Age Pages — informative fact sheets for older people. There are over 40 titles in the series, many of which are available in Spanish.

Long-distance caregivers might find the following titles of particular interest:

- "Home Safety for People with Alzheimer's Disease"
- "Good Nutrition: It's a Way of Life"
- "Older Drivers"
- "Caregiver Guide: Tips for Caregivers of People with Alzheimer's Disease"
- "Long-Term Care: Choosing the Right Place"

SOME GOOD IDEAS

Know what you need to know. Experienced caregivers recommend that you learn as much as you can about your parent's illness and treatment. Information can help you understand what is going on, anticipate the course of an illness, prevent crises, and assist in disease management. It can also make talking with the doctor easier. Learn as much as you can about the resources available. Make sure at least one family member has written permission to receive medical and financial information. Try putting together a notebook, or something similar, that includes all the vital information about health care, social services, contact numbers, financial issues, and so on. Make copies for other caregivers.

Plan your visits. When visiting your parent, you may feel that there is just too much to do in the time that you have. You can get more done and feel less stressed by talking to your parent ahead of time and finding out what he or she would like to do. This may help you set clear-cut and realistic goals for the visit. For instance, does your mother need to go to the mall or to visit another family member? Could your father use help fixing things around the house? Would you like to talk to your mother's physician? Decide on the priorities and leave other tasks to another visit.

Remember to actually spend time visiting with your family member. Try to make time to do things unrelated to being a caregiver. Maybe you could rent a movie to watch with your parents, or visit with old friends or other family members. Perhaps your aunt or uncle would like to attend worship services. Offer to play a game of cards or a board game. Take a drive, or go to the library together. Finding a little bit of time to do something simple and relaxing can help everyone.

Get in touch and stay in touch. Many families schedule conference calls with doctors, the assisted living facility team, or nursing home staff to get up-to-date information about a parent's health and progress. If your parent is in a nursing home, you can request occasional teleconferences with the facility's staff. Some families schedule conference calls so several relatives can participate in one conversation. Sometimes a social worker is good to talk to for updates as well as for help in making decisions. The human touch is important too. Try to find people in your parent's community who can be your eyes and ears and provide a realistic view of what is going on. In some cases, this will be your other parent.

Help your parent stay in contact. For one family, having a private phone line installed in their father's nursing home room allowed him to stay in touch. For another family, giving the grandmother a cell phone (and then teaching her to use it) gave everyone some peace of mind. You can program telephone numbers (such as doctors,' neighbors,' and your own) into your parent's phone so that he or she can speed-dial contacts. Such simple strategies can be a lifeline for you and your parent. But be prepared — you may find you are inundated with calls from your parent. It's good to think in advance about a workable approach for coping with numerous calls.

Get a phone book, either hardcopy or online, that lists resources in your parent's neighborhood. Having a copy of the phone book for your parent's city or town can be really helpful. The "Blue Pages" can provide an easy guide to State and local services available in your parent's hometown.

4. How Can My Family Decide Who Does What?

Be sure to talk with other family members and decide who will be responsible for which tasks. Think about your schedules and how to adapt them to give respite to a primary caregiver or to coordinate holiday and vacation times. One family found that it worked to have the long-distance caregiver come to town while the primary caregiver was on a family vacation. And remember, if you aren't the primary caregiver, offering appreciation, reassurance, and positive feedback is also a contribution.

KNOW YOUR STRENGTHS/SET YOUR LIMITS

If you decide to work as a family team, it makes sense to agree in advance how your skills can complement one another. Ideally, each of you will be able to take on tasks best suited to each person's skills or interests. For example, who is available to help Mom get to the grocery store each week? Who can help Dad organize his move to an assisted living facility? After making these kinds of decisions, remember that over time responsibilities may need to be revised to reflect changes in the situation or your parent's needs. Be realistic about how much you can do and what you are willing to do.

When thinking about your strengths, consider what you are particularly good at and how that skill might help in the current situation:

- Are you best on the phone, finding information, keeping people up-to-date on changing conditions, and offering cheer?
- Are you good at supervising and leading others?
- Are you comfortable speaking with medical staff and interpreting what they say to others?
- Is your strongest suit doing the numbers— paying bills, keeping track of bank statements, and reviewing insurance policies and reimbursement reports?

WHEN REFLECTING ON YOUR LIMITS, CONSIDER:

- How often, both mentally and financially, can you afford to travel?
- Are you emotionally prepared to take on what may feel like a reversal of roles between you and your parent — and to respect your parent's autonomy?
- Can you be both calm and assertive when communicating from a distance?
- How will your decision to take on care responsibilities affect the rest of your family and your work?

5. Are There Things I Can Do That Will Help Me Feel Less Frustrated? What Can I Do to Take Care of Myself?

Feeling frustrated and angry with everyone, from your parent to his or her doctors, is a common caregiving experience. It can be hard to acknowledge that you feel this way, but try not to criticize yourself even more. Caregiving, especially from a distance, is likely to bring out a full range of human emotions, both positive and negative. If you feel angry, it could be a sign that you are overwhelmed or that you are trying to do too much. If you can, give yourself a break: Take a walk, talk with your friends, get some sleep, join a support group — try to do something for yourself.

Consider joining a caregiver support group, either in your own community or online. Meeting other caregivers can relieve your sense of isolation and will give you a chance to exchange stories and ideas. By focusing on what you can do, you may be able to free yourself from some of the worry and focus on being supportive and loving.

Most caregivers report feeling guilty about almost everything — about not being closer, not doing enough, not having enough time. Worrying about being able to afford to take time off from work or the cost of travel can increase frustration.

6. What Is a Geriatric Care Manager and How Can I Find One?

Professional care managers are usually licensed nursing or social work professionals who specialize in geriatrics. Some families hire a geriatric care manager to evaluate and assess a parent's needs and to coordinate care through community resources. The cost of an initial evaluation varies and may be expensive, but geriatric care managers can offer a useful service. They are a sort of "professional relative" to help you and your family to identify needs and how to meet them. These professionals can also be helpful in leading family discussions about sensitive subjects.

When interviewing a geriatric care manager, you might want to ask:

- Are you a licensed geriatric care manager?
- Are you a member of the National Association of Professional Geriatric Care Managers?
- How long have you been providing care management services?
- Are you available for emergencies?
- Does your company also provide home care services?
- How will you communicate information to me?
- What are your fees? Will you provide them in writing prior to starting services?
- Can you provide references?

The National Association of Professional Geriatric Care Managers can help you find a care manager near your family member's community. You can also contact the Eldercare Locator for recommendations. In some cases, local chapters of the Alzheimer's Association may be able to recommend geriatric care managers who have assisted other families.

7. How Can I Keep Up
with My Parent's Medical Care?
I Don't Know Where to Start.

Health care experts recommend that you start by learning as much as you can about your parent's illness, current treatments, and its likely course. This information will be essential as you help your parent and the primary caregiver cope with day-to-day concerns, make decisions, and plan for the future.

When you visit your parent, consider going along on a doctor's appointment (check that your parent does not mind having you there). Some long-distance caregivers say that making a separate appointment with a doctor allows them to seek more detailed information and answers to questions. These appointments must be paid for out-of-pocket.

You must have permission to have any conversation with your parent's doctor. Ask your parent to complete a release form that allows the doctor to discuss his or her health care with you. Be sure the release is up-to-date and that there's a copy in your parent's records in addition to keeping a back-up copy for your files.

8. How Can I Make the Most of a
Visit with My Parent's Doctor?
I Don't Want to Waste the Doctor's Time.

If you go with your parent to see the doctor, here are a few tips that will help you be an ally and advocate:

- Bring a prioritized list of questions and take notes on what the doctor recommends. Both can be helpful later, either to give information to the primary caregiver, or to remind your parent what the doctor said.
- Before the appointment, ask your parent, the primary caregiver, and your siblings if they have any questions or concerns they would like you to bring up.
- Bring a list of ALL medications your parent is taking, both prescription and over-the-counter, and include dosage and schedule (if your parent sees several different doctors one may not necessarily know what another has prescribed).
- When the doctor asks a question, do not answer for your parent unless you have been asked to do so. Always talk to the doctor and to your parent.

145

- Respect your parent's privacy, and leave the room when necessary.

- Ask the doctor if she or he can recommend community resources that might be helpful.

- Larger medical practices and hospitals may have a social worker on staff. Ask to speak with the social worker. She or he may have valuable information about community resources.

NIA has a free booklet called *Talking with Your Doctor: A Guide for Older People* that provides helpful information about doctor/patient communication. It includes hints on getting ready for a doctor's appointment, making health care decisions, and talking about sensitive subjects.

9. How on Earth Can My Parents Afford Everything They Need? They Saved Money for Retirement, but the Cost of Their Health Care Is Really High.

You are not alone in worrying about how much everything costs. Health care expenses can be crushing, even for middle-class families who thought they had saved enough. Your parents may be eligible for some health care benefits. People on fixed incomes who have limited resources may qualify for Medicaid, a program of the Centers for Medicare and Medicaid Services (CMS), a Federal agency. CMS covers the costs of health care for people of all ages who meet income requirements and who are disabled. Because the guidelines change often, you should check with CMS regularly.

Medicare offers insurance for prescription drugs. For information about this coverage, visit www.medicare.gov or call 1-800-MEDICARE (1-800-633-4227).

The State Health Insurance Assistance Program (SHIP) is a national program offering one-on-one counseling and assistance to people and their families on Medicare. SHIPs provide free counseling and assistance to Medicare beneficiaries on a wide range of Medicare, Medicaid, and Medigap matters. To find your State program, visit www.shipusa.org.

If prescription medications cost too much, talk to the doctor about the possibility of prescribing a less expensive medication. The Partnership for Prescription Assistance can provide a list of patient assistance programs supported by pharmaceutical companies.

10. What Kinds of Documents Do We Need? It Sounds Like Caregiving Requires a Lot of Paperwork.

Effective caregiving depends on keeping a great deal of information in order and up-to-date. Often, long-distance caregivers will need to have information about a parent's personal, health, financial, and legal records. If you have ever tried to gather and organize your own personal information, you know what a chore it can be. Gathering and organizing this information from far away can seem even more challenging. Maintaining up-to-date information about your parent's health and medical care, as well as finances, home ownership, and other legal issues, lets you get a handle on what is going on and allows you to respond quickly if there is a crisis.

If you do not see your parent often, one visit may not be enough time for you to get all the paperwork organized. Instead, try to focus on gathering the essentials first; you can fill in the blanks as you go along. You might begin by talking to your parent and his or her primary caregiver about the kinds of records that need to be pulled together. If a primary caregiver is already on the scene, chances are that some of the information has already been assembled. Talk about any missing information or documentation and how you might help to organize the records.

Your parents may be reluctant to share personal information with you. Explain that you are not trying to invade their privacy or take over their personal lives — you are only trying to assemble what they (and you) will need in the event of an emergency. Assure them that you will respect their privacy and keep your promise. If your parents are still uncomfortable, ask if they would be willing to work with an attorney (some lawyers specialize in elder affairs) or perhaps with another trusted family member or friend.

11. Should I Encourage My Parents to Get More Help?

If you do not see your parent often, changes in his or her health may seem dramatic. In contrast, the primary caregiver might not notice such changes, or realize that more help, medical treatment, or supervision is needed. Sometimes a geriatric care manager or other professional is the first to notice changes. For families dealing with Alzheimer's disease and other dementias, it can be easier to "cover" for the patient — doing things for him or her, filling in information in conversations, and so on — than to acknowledge what is happening.

Some changes may not be what you think. Occasional forgetfulness does not necessarily indicate Alzheimer's disease. Before you raise the issue of what needs to be done, talk to your parent and the primary caregiver about your concerns. Try not to sound critical when you raise the subject. Instead, mention your particular worry and explain why you are concerned. Listen to what the primary caregiver says about the situation, and whether he or she feels there are problems.

Discuss what you think needs to be done: "Do we need to get a second opinion about the diagnosis? Can you follow the medication schedule? Would you like some help with housework?" Try to follow up your suggestions with practical help, and give specific examples of what you can do. For example, you might arrange to have a personal or home health aide come in once a week. You might schedule doctors' appointments or arrange for transportation.

In some cases you may have to be forceful, especially if you feel that the situation is unhealthy or unsafe. Do not leave a frail adult at risk. If you have to act against the wishes of your parent or the primary caregiver, be direct and explain what you are going to do. Discuss your plan and say why you are taking action.

12. How Can We Make the House Safer for My Mother Who Has Alzheimer's Disease? I'm Worried About Her Safety.

You can take many precautions that will make the house safer, more accessible, and comfortable. Because you are not present, you may want to evaluate the safety of your mother's home during one of your visits (with the understanding that you must quickly correct any real dangers). On future visits, you should be alert for hazards and aware of things you can do to make the house safer.

If you are worried about your parent's safety, don't wait until the next visit. If you feel that your parent is unsafe alone, make note of which behaviors have become most worrisome and discuss these with the primary caregiver and the doctor. Behavior that is unsafe or unhealthy may have become familiar to the primary caregiver. The kitchen in particular presents many opportunities for accidents, especially when a parent misuses appliances or forgets that something is cooking. Discuss your concerns and offer to help adapt the environment to meet your parent's changing safety needs.

If you are concerned about home safety for a parent who has Alzheimer's disease, NIA's free pamphlet, *Home Safety for People with Alzheimer's Disease* has plenty of helpful suggestions.

Consider these principles about home safety for older people:

1. Think prevention. It is hard to predict or anticipate every problem, but you can go through the house room-by-room and evaluate safety problems. Checking the safety of your parent's home may prevent a hazardous situation. Some easy steps to take:

   • Remind the primary caregiver to lock all doors and windows on the inside and outside to prevent wandering.
   • Make sure all potentially harmful items, such as medications, weapons, machinery, or electrical cords are put away in a safe, preferably locked place when they're not in use, and when necessary.
   • Use child-resistant caps on medicine bottles and childproof door latches on storage units as well.

2. Adapt the environment. Because it is easier to change a place than to change a person, consider the following:

   • Install at least one stairway handrail that extends beyond the first and last steps.
   • Place carpet or safety grip strips on stairs.
   • Avoid clutter, which can cause disorientation and confusion.
   • Keep all walk areas free of furniture, and extension and electrical cords.
   • Cover unused outlets with childproof plugs.
   • Make sure all rooms have adequate lighting.

13. How Can I Help Lighten the Load for My Mother?

Your mother may be hesitant to ask for help, or to say that she needs a break. Be sure to acknowledge how important her care has been for your father. Also discuss the physical and emotional effects caregiving can have on people. True, care-giving can be satisfying, but it also can be very hard work. Offer to help arrange for respite care.

Respite care will give your mother a break from her caregiving responsibilities. Respite care can be for an afternoon or for several days. Care can be provided in the family home, or your dad may spend the time in an adult day services program or at a skilled nursing facility. The ARCH National Respite Locator Service can help you to find services in your parent's community.

You might suggest your mother contact the Well Spouse Association — it offers support to the wives, husbands, and partners of chronically ill or disabled people and has a nationwide listing of local groups.

Your parents may need more help from home-based care to continue to live in their own home. Some people find it hard to have paid caregivers in the house but most also say that the help is invaluable. If your mother is reluctant, point out that with in-home help she may have more energy to devote to your father's care and some time for herself.

Over time, your father may need to move to assisted living or a nursing home. If that happens, try to support your mother. You can help her select a facility. She may need help adjusting to his absence or to living alone in their home. Just listening may not sound like much help, but often it is.

14. How Can I Help My Folks Decide If It's Time for Them to Move?

The decision about whether your parents should move is often tricky and emotional. Each family will have its own reasons for wanting (or not wanting) to take such a step. One family may decide a move is right because the parents no longer need so much space or cannot manage the home. For another family the need for hands-on care in a long-term care facility motivates a change. In some cases, a move frees up cash so that the parent can afford a more suitable situation.

In the case of long-distance caregivers, the notion of moving can seem like a solution to the problem of not being close enough to help. For some caregivers, moving a sick or aging parent to their own home or community can be a viable alternative. In some cases, an adult child moves back to the parent's home to become the primary caregiver. Keep in mind that leaving a home, community, and familiar medical care can be very disruptive and difficult.

Older adults and their families have some choices when it comes to deciding where to live, but these choices can be limited by factors such as illness, financial resources, and personal preferences. Making a decision that is best for your parent — and making that decision with your parent — can be difficult. Try to learn as much as you can about possible housing options.

Older adults, or those with serious illness, can:

- stay in their own home, or move to a smaller one,
- move to an assisted living facility or retirement community,
- move to a long-term care facility, or
- move in with another family member.

Experts advise families to think carefully before moving an aging adult into an adult child's home. In its fact sheet "Home Away From Home," the Family

Caregiver Alliance suggests considering the following issues before deciding whether or not to move your parent to your home:

- Evaluate whether your parent needs constant supervision or assistance throughout the day, and consider how this will be provided.
- Identify which activities of daily living (eating, bathing, toileting) your parent can perform independently.
- Determine your comfort level for providing personal care such as bathing or changing an adult diaper.
- Take an honest look at your health and physical abilities, and decide if you are able to provide care for your parent.
- Expect changes in your parent's medical or cognitive condition.
- Explore the availability of services such as a friendly visitor, in-home care, or adult day services.
- Investigate back-up options if living with your parent does not work or is not your choice.
- Consider the type of medical care your parent needs and find out if appropriate doctors and services are available in your community.

15. What Happens If My Mother Gets Too Sick to Stay at Home?

If you are over 40, chances are you've had a similar conversation with someone you love. It might come up if you see a segment about nursing homes while watching the evening news. "Promise you'll never send me to a nursing home," your mother says. This request usually reflects what most of us want: to stay in our own homes, to maintain independence, to turn to family and friends for help.

Sometimes, however, parents really do want their adult children to make a promise. Think carefully before doing so. According to the Centers for Medicare and Medicaid Services, "Quality of care means doing the right thing, at the right time, in the right way, for the right person, and having the best possible results." Agreeing that you will not "put someone" in a nursing home may close the door to the right care option for your family. It requires you to know that no matter what happens you will be able to care for your parent. The fact is that for some illnesses, and for some people, professional health care in a long-term care facility is the only reasonable choice.

When faced with a parent who is truly ill or frail, long-distance caregivers may find that some promises hamper their ability to do what is necessary, either for their own health, or for their parent's. Many people discover too late that the promises they made ("Of course you will be able to die at home.") cannot be kept.

Try to focus your commitments on what you know here and now. If asked to make a promise, you could say something like, "Dad, I will make sure you have the best care we can arrange. You can count on me to try and do what's best for everyone. I can't think of a situation where I'd walk out on you." Base your promises and decisions on a realistic assessment of the current situation or diagnosis, and realize that you may need to revisit your agreement. Your father's situation might change. Your situation might change. You truly do not know what will happen in the future — disease and illness can lead to enormous changes. And, of course, it's not only your parent's health that changes — your own health may alter over time, too.

If you've already made a promise to a parent, remember you can bring the subject up again; you can change your answer to something more specific, something you feel you can undertake. As hard as that conversation might be, it may be better than risking the guilt of a promise not kept.

16. How Is It That Long-Distance Caregiving Makes Me Feel So Guilty All the Time?

You might think that being far away gives you some immunity from feeling overwhelmed by what is happening to your parent — but long-distance caregivers report that this is not so. Although you may not feel as physically exhausted and drained as the primary, hands-on caregiver, you may still feel worried and anxious. Many long-distance caregivers describe feeling terribly guilty about not being there, about not being able to do enough or spend enough time with the parent. Remind yourself that you are doing the best you can given the circumstances, and you can only do what you can do.

If you are like most long-distance caregivers, you already have many people who rely on you: Your spouse, children, perhaps even grandchildren, as well as friends, coworkers, and colleagues. Adding one more "to-do" to your list may seem impossible.

You may find some consolation or comfort in knowing that you are not alone. Many people find that support groups are a great resource and a way to learn caregiving tips and techniques that work — even from a distance. Others find the camaraderie and companionship helpful. Some enjoy meeting monthly or weekly, while others find what they need in online support groups. The Eldercare Locator may be able to help you find a local group. This booklet has details on how to contact organizations that may have helpful information.

17. How Can I Be Sure That My Father's Caregiver Isn't Mistreating Him?

From a distance, it can be hard to assess the quality of your father's caregivers. Ideally, if there is a primary caregiver on the scene, he or she can keep tabs on how things are going. Sometimes a geriatric care manager can help. You can stay in touch by phone and take note of any concerns that might indicate neglect or mistreatment. These can happen in any setting, at any socioeconomic level. They can take many forms, including domestic violence, emotional abuse, financial abuse, and basic neglect.

The stress that may happen when adult children care for their aging parents can take a toll on everyone. In some families, abuse continues a long-standing family pattern. In others, the older adult's need for constant care can cause a caregiver to lash out verbally or physically. In some cases, especially in the mid-to-late stages of Alzheimer's disease, the older adult may become physically aggressive and difficult to manage. This might cause a caregiver to respond angrily. But no matter what the cause or who is the perpetrator, abuse and neglect are never acceptable responses.

If you feel that your parent is in physical danger, contact the authorities right away. If you suspect abuse, but do not feel there is an immediate risk, contact someone who can act on your behalf: your parent's doctor, for instance, or your contact at a home health agency. Suspected abuse must be reported to adult protective services.

ELDER MISTREATMENT

Elder mistreatment is the intentional or unintentional hurting, either physical or emotional, of an older person. Some signs to watch for:

- Bruises, pressure marks, broken bones, abrasions, and burns may indicate physical abuse, neglect, or mistreatment.
- Unexplained withdrawal from normal activities, a sudden change in alertness, and unusual depression may indicate emotional abuse.
- Sudden changes in financial situations may be the result of exploitation.
- Bedsores, unattended medical needs, poor hygiene, and unusual, unexplained weight loss can indicate neglect.
- Behavior such as belittling, threats, and other uses of power and control by spouses may indicate verbal or emotional abuse.
- Strained or tense relationships, and frequent arguments between the caregiver and older person can indicate mistreatment.

If your parent is in a long-term care facility, the facility must take steps to prevent (and report) abuse. Nursing homes, like hospitals, are subject to strict state licensing requirements and federal regulations. Even so, neglect and abuse can occur. For more information, contact the National Center on Elder Abuse.

SIGNS OF SELF-NEGLECT

Self-neglect describes situations in which older people put themselves at high risk. People who neglect themselves may have a disorder which impairs their judgment or memory. They may have a chronic disease. Knowing where to draw the line between self-neglect and a person's right to independence can be hard. Here are some signs that may mean it's time to intervene:

- Hoarding (Diogenes syndrome, syllogomania)
- Failure to take essential medications or refusal to seek medical treatment for serious illness
- Leaving a burning stove unattended
- Poor hygiene
- Not wearing suitable clothing for the weather
- Confusion
- Inability to attend to housekeeping
- Dehydration

18. How Can I Help My Parents Think About Their Future Health Care Preferences?

Making advance care plans is a key step for your parent to take to be sure that his or her health care preferences are known. Health care providers can only respect those wishes that have been made known and are documented in the medical record. Advance care planning can help your family avoid some of the conflicts that can occur when family members disagree over treatment decisions.

It may be easier to make certain decisions after discussing them with family, clergy members, or health care providers. Decisions about forgoing treatment, for instance, or ending life support, involve complex emotional issues and are hard for many people to make alone. Try to make peace with yourself and your family, whatever the decision. As one caregiver put it, "So much of the task is wading through your own feelings—and the rest is just figuring out what to do."

When thinking about the future consider:

- Naming a surrogate decision maker (a surrogate has the authority to make decisions on behalf of someone who is too ill to do so),
- Stating which treatment results are desirable and which ones are unacceptable,
- Discussing what to do in an emergency,
- Noting preferences regarding any possible treatments, and whether or not a time-limited trial would be acceptable (for instance, 5 days on a ventilator to recover some strength; a week with a feeding tube, and so on),
- Talking to the doctor and surrogate about preferences and including written instructions in the medical record.

Advance care planning is an ongoing process. As an illness progresses and circumstances change, your parent may want to revisit his or her preferences. If so, be sure to update all written instructions and share the changes with health care providers and anyone who assists with care.

Try to approach decision-making tasks by recognizing that you are working with a parent, not for a parent (unless you are healthcare proxy or agent, in which case, you will be implementing a family member's decisions). How will you know when the advance care plans are complete and that you have covered all the bases? A complete plan will:

- be very specific and detailed and cover what is to be done in a variety of medical situations,
- name a healthcare proxy,
- be recorded in the medical record, and
- be readily available to any caregiver in the home, nursing home, or hospital.

19. What Is the Difference Between an Advance Directive and a Living Will?

Advance directives are oral and written instructions about future medical care should your parent become unable to make decisions (for example, unconscious or too ill to communicate). Each State regulates the use of advance directives differently. A living will is one type of advance directive. It takes effect when the patient is terminally ill.

Advance directives are not set in stone. A patient can revise and update the contents as often as he or she wishes. Patients and caregivers should discuss these decisions—and any changes in them—and keep the health care team informed.

Everyone involved should be aware of your parents' treatment preferences. Because State laws vary, check with your Area Agency on Aging, a lawyer, or financial planner. They may have information on wills, trusts, estates, inheritance taxes, insurance, Medicare, and Medicaid.

The person who has the authority to make medical decisions on another person's behalf is called a healthcare proxy. The terms "healthcare proxy" and "healthcare agent" or "surrogate" are used interchangeably. These responsibilities are called "durable" (for example, you may hear the phrase "durable power of attorney") because they remain in effect even if your parent is unable to make decisions. Most people appoint a close friend or family member. Some people turn to a trusted member of the clergy or a lawyer. The designated person should be able to understand the treatment choices. Know your parents' values, and support their decisions.

The decision to name a healthcare proxy is extremely important. A written document, kept in the medical record and identifying the designated proxy, should always be up-to-date.

Durable medical power of attorney forms do not give explicit guidance to the proxy about what decisions to make. Many States have developed forms that combine the intent of the durable power of attorney (to have an advocate) and the intent of the living will (to state choices for treatment at the end of life). These combination forms may be more effective than either of the two used individually. Each State regulates advance directives differently, so you will need to consult with the physician, nurse, social worker, or family lawyer to know what is required. It's also a good idea to check to make sure that all financial matters, including wills and life insurance policies, are in order.

What Other Information Should I Keep Track Of?

The answer to this question is different for every family. You might want to help organize the following information and update it as needed. This list is just a starting point.

- Full legal name and residence
- Birth date and place
- Social Security number
- Employer(s) and dates of employment
- Education and military records
- Sources of income and assets; investment income (stocks, bonds, property)

- Insurance policies, bank accounts, deeds, investments, and other valuables
- Most recent income tax return
- Money owed, to whom, and when payments are due
- Credit card and charge account names and numbers

20. What If I'm Told Mom Only Has a Few Months to Live?

The news that a family member is dying is difficult to bear — and yet, it is a basic part of life. When you hear that a parent has a terminal illness, you may be flooded with emotions: Sorrow, disbelief, anger, anxiety. It can be hard to know what to do or what to say. Fortunately, many organizations are working to improve the lives of dying people and their families. Try to locate a hospice program. Hospice provides special care for people who are near the end of life. Check with Medicare for information on hospice benefits.

Talk to your own friends, clergy, or colleagues. Just about everyone has experienced the serious illness and death of a beloved friend or family member. Exchanging stories can help you as you cope with your own loss and with trying to decide what you can do.

Contact your parent's doctor and talk to your own doctor as well to find out what will need to be done, the kinds of care that your mother or father is likely to need, and how you can arrange for it to happen.

Some people find that it is very hard to talk about death and dying, and will go to great lengths to avoid the subject. Difficult as it is, talk to your parents about what is going on, but if you can't have that conversation, don't let that add to your worry. There is no single "right" way to approach the death of a loved one.

Appendix C

Caring for the Caregiver

This booklet was published by the National Cancer Institute, U.S. Department of Health and Human Services on June 29, 2007. The full text of the publication can be read or downloaded from http://www.cancer.gov/cancertopics/caring-for-the-caregiver. It was prepared for caregivers of patients with cancer; however much of the content is relevant to any caregiver.

WHO IS A CAREGIVER?

Are you helping a loved one get through cancer treatment? If you are, then this booklet is for you. You are a "caregiver."

You may not think of yourself as a caregiver. You may feel you are doing something natural. You are just caring for someone you love. Some caregivers are family members. Others are friends.

What Does "Giving Care" Mean?

Giving care can mean helping with daily needs. These include going to doctor visits, making meals, and picking up medicines. It can also mean helping your loved one cope with feelings. Like when he or she feels sad or angry. Sometimes having someone to talk to is what your loved one needs most.

While giving care, it's normal to put your own needs and feelings aside. But putting your needs aside for a long time is not good for your health. You need to take care of yourself, too. If you don't, you may not be able to care for others. This is why you need to take good care of *you*.

YOUR FEELINGS

It's common to feel stressed and overwhelmed at this time. Like your loved one, you may feel angry, sad, or worried. Try to share your feelings with others who can help you. It can help to talk about how you feel. You could even talk to a counselor or social worker.

Understanding Your Feelings

You probably have many feelings as you take care of your loved one. There is no right way for you to feel. Each person is different.

The first step to understanding your feelings is to know that they're normal. Give yourself some time to think through them. Some feelings that may come and go are:

- *Sadness.* It's okay to feel sad. But if it lasts for more than 2 weeks, and it keeps you from doing what you need to do, you may be depressed.
- *Anger.* You may be angry at yourself or family members. You may be angry at the person you're caring for. Or you may be angry that your loved one has cancer. Sometimes anger comes from fear, panic, or stress. If you are angry, try to think of what makes you feel this way. Knowing the cause may help.
- *Grief.* You may be feeling a loss of what you value most. This may be your loved one's health. Or it may be the loss of the day-to-day life you had before the cancer was found. Let yourself grieve these losses.
- *Guilt.* Feeling guilty is common, too. You may think you aren't helping enough. Or you may feel guilty that you are healthy.
- *Loneliness.* You can feel lonely, even with lots of people around you. You may feel that no one understands your problems. You may also be spending less time with others.

What May Help

Talk with someone if your feelings get in the way of daily life. Maybe you have a family member, friend, priest, pastor, or spiritual leader to talk to. Your doctor may also be able to help.

Here are some other things that may help you:

- Know that we all make mistakes whenever we have a lot on our minds. No one is perfect.

- Cry or express your feelings. You don't have to pretend to be cheerful. It's okay to show that you are sad or upset.
- Focus on things that are worth your time and energy. Let small things go for now. For example, don't fold clothes if you are tired.
- Remind yourself that you are doing the best you can.
- Spend time alone to think about your feelings.

ASKING FOR HELP

Many people who were once caregivers say they did too much on their own. Some wished that they had asked for help sooner. Be honest about what you can do. Think about tasks you can give to others. And let go of tasks that aren't so important at this time.

Asking for Help Also Helps Your Loved One

Don't be afraid to ask for help. Remember, if you get help for yourself:

- You may stay healthier and have more energy.
- Your loved one may feel less guilty about your help.
- Other helpers may offer time and skills that you don't have.

How Can Others Help You?

People may want to help you but don't know what you need. Here are some things you can ask them to do:

1. Help with everyday tasks.
2. Talk with you and share your feelings.
3. Help with driving errands.
4. Find information you need.
5. Tell others how your loved one is doing.

Know That Some People May Say, "No."

Some people may not be able to help. There could be one or more reasons such as:

- They may be coping with their own problems.
- They may not have time right now.
- They may not know how to help.
- They may feel uneasy around people who are sick.

CARING FOR YOURSELF

Making Time for Yourself

Taking time for yourself can help you be a better caregiver. That's even more true if you have health problems. You may want to:

- Find nice things you can do for yourself. Even just a few minutes can help. You could watch TV, call a friend, work on a hobby, or do anything that you enjoy.
- Be active. Even light exercise such as walking, stretching, or dancing can make you less tired. Yard work, playing with children or pets, or working in the garden are helpful, too.
- Find ways to connect with friends. Are there places you can meet others who are close to you? Or can you chat or get support by phone or email?
- Give yourself more time off. Ask friends or family members to pitch in. Take time to rest.

Do something for yourself each day. It doesn't matter how small it is. Whatever you do, don't neglect yourself.

Joining a Caregiver Support Group

In a support group for caregivers, people may talk about their feelings and trade advice. Others may just want to listen. You can talk things over with other caregivers. This could give you some ideas for coping. It may also help you know you aren't alone.

In many cities, support groups are held in other languages besides English. There are also groups that meet over the Internet. Ask a nurse or a social worker to help you find a support group that meets your needs.

Caring for Your Body

You may feel too busy to think about your own health. But taking care of your body gives you strength. Then you can take care of someone else.

Keep up with your own health needs. Try to:

- Go to all your checkups.
- Get enough rest.
- Take your medications.
- Exercise.
- Eat healthy meals.
- Make time to relax.

Did you have health problems before you became a caregiver? If so, now it's even more important to take care of yourself. Also, adding extra stressors to your life can cause new health problems. Be sure to tell your doctor if you notice any new changes in your body.

TALKING WITH OTHERS

Your Partner or Spouse

Nearly all caregivers and their partners feel more stress than usual in their relationship. They must deal with many decisions and changes. Some couples find that their bonds get stronger during cancer treatment. Others find they get weaker.

- Try to be open about your stress and its causes.
- Talk about how each of you feels.
- Share how you are each coping.
- Look at things that are causing you both stress.
- Talk about choices you can make together.
- Try to be grateful for each other.
- Make time to focus on things.

Talk with the people close to you. Try to be open and caring. Ask a counselor to hold a family meeting if needed. During stressful times, ask someone else to update others about how your loved one is doing.

Dealing with Help You Don't Need

Sometimes people offer help you don't need. Thank them for their concern. Tell them you'll let them know if you need anything.

Some people may offer unwanted advice. They may do this because they don't know what else to say. It's up to you to decide how to deal with this. You don't have to respond at all. Otherwise, thank them and let it go. Tell them you are taking steps to help your family.

As a Caregiver, Try to Remember to:

• Strike a balance each day.
• Focus on your needs, too.
• Care for yourself while caring for your loved one.
• Make time for resting and relaxing.

Life-changing events often give people the chance to grow. They may help people see what's most important to them. Many say that caring for someone with cancer changed them forever. They used their strengths to support their loved one. And they learned more about themselves along the way.

Appendix D

Tips for Caregivers of People with Alzheimer's Disease

TIPS FOR CAREGIVERS

Caring for a person with Alzheimer's disease (AD) at home is a difficult task and can become overwhelming at times. Each day brings new challenges as the caregiver copes with changing levels of ability and new patterns of behavior. Research has shown that caregivers themselves often are at increased risk for depression and illness, especially if they do not receive adequate support from family, friends, and the community.

One of the biggest struggles caregivers face is dealing with the difficult behaviors of the person they are caring for. Dressing, bathing, eating — basic activities of daily living — often become difficult to manage for both the person with AD and the caregiver. Having a plan for getting through the day can help caregivers cope. Many caregivers have found it helpful to use strategies for dealing with difficult behaviors and stressful situations. Through trial and error you will find that some of the following tips work, while others do not. Each person with AD is unique and will respond differently, and each person changes over the course of the disease. Do the best you can, and remind yourself to take breaks.

DEALING WITH THE DIAGNOSIS

Finding out that a loved one has Alzheimer's disease can be stressful, frightening, and overwhelming. As you begin to take stock of the situation, here are some tips that may help:

- Ask the doctor any questions you have about AD. Find out what treatments might work best to alleviate symptoms or address behavior problems.

- Contact organizations such as the Alzheimer's Association and the Alzheimer's Disease Education and Referral (ADEAR) Center for more information about the disease, treatment options, and caregiving resources. Some community groups may offer classes to teach caregiving, problem-solving, and management skills. Find a support group where you can share your feelings and concerns. Members of support groups often have helpful ideas or know of useful resources based on their own experiences. Online support groups make it possible for caregivers to receive support without having to leave home.

- Study your day to see if you can develop a routine that makes things go more smoothly. If there are times of day when the person with AD is less confused or more cooperative, plan your routine to make the most of those moments. Keep in mind that the way the person functions may change from day to day, so try to be flexible and adapt your routine as needed.

- Consider using adult day care or respite services to ease the day-to-day demands of caregiving. These services allow you to have a break while knowing that the person with AD is being well cared for.

- Begin to plan for the future. This may include getting financial and legal documents in order, investigating long-term care options, and determining what services are covered by health insurance and Medicare.

COMMUNICATION

Trying to communicate with a person who has AD can be a challenge. Both understanding and being understood may be difficult.

- Choose simple words and short sentences and use a gentle, calm tone of voice.

- Avoid talking to the person with AD like a baby or talking about the person as if he or she were not there.

- Minimize distractions and noise — such as the television or radio— to help the person focus on what you are saying.

- Call the person by name, making sure you have his or her attention before speaking.

- Allow enough time for a response. Be careful not to interrupt.
- If the person with AD is struggling to find a word or communicate a thought, gently try to provide the word he or she is looking for.
- Try to frame questions and instructions in a positive way.

BATHING

While some people with AD don't mind bathing, for others it is a frightening, confusing experience. Advance planning can help make bath time better for both of you.

- Plan the bath or shower for the time of day when the person is most calm and agreeable. Be consistent. Try to develop a routine.
- Respect the fact that bathing is scary and uncomfortable for some people with AD. Be gentle and respectful. Be patient and calm.
- Tell the person what you are going to do, step by step, and allow him or her to do as much as possible.
- Prepare in advance. Make sure you have everything you need ready and in the bathroom before beginning. Draw the bath ahead of time, but do not let the water become too cool.
- Be sensitive to the temperature. Warm up the room beforehand if necessary and keep extra towels and a robe nearby. Test the water temperature before beginning the bath or shower.
- Minimize safety risks by using a handheld showerhead, shower bench, grab bars, and nonskid bath mats. *Never* leave the person alone in the bath or shower.
- Try a sponge bath. Bathing may not be necessary every day. A sponge bath can be effective between showers or baths.

DRESSING

For someone who has AD, getting dressed presents a series of challenges: choosing what to wear, getting some clothes off and other clothes on, and struggling with buttons and zippers. Minimizing the challenges may make a difference.

- Try to have the person get dressed at the same time each day so he or she will come to expect it as part of the daily routine.

- Encourage the person to dress himself or herself to whatever degree possible. Plan to allow extra time so there is no pressure or rush.

- Allow the person to choose from a limited selection of outfits. If he or she has a favorite outfit, consider buying several identical sets.

- Arrange the clothes in the order they are to be put on to help the person move through the process.

- Provide clear, step-by-step instructions if the person needs prompting.

- Choose clothing that is comfortable, easy to put on and take off, and easy to care for. Elastic waists and Velcro enclosures minimize struggles with buttons and zippers.

EATING

Eating can be a challenge. Some people with AD want to eat all the time, while others have to be encouraged to maintain a good diet.

- View mealtimes as opportunities for social interaction and success for the person with AD. Try to be patient and avoid rushing, and be sensitive to confusion and anxiety.

- Aim for a quiet, calm, reassuring mealtime atmosphere by limiting noise and other distractions.

- Maintain familiar mealtime routines, but adapt to the person's changing needs.

- Give the person food choices, but limit the number of choices. Try to offer appealing foods that have familiar flavors, varied textures, and different colors.

- Serve small portions or several small meals throughout the day. Make healthy snacks, finger foods, and shakes available. In the earlier stages of dementia, be aware of the possibility of overeating.

- Choose dishes and eating tools that promote independence. If the person has trouble using utensils, use a bowl instead of a plate, or offer utensils with large or built-up handles. Use straws or cups with lids to make drinking easier.

- Encourage the person to drink plenty of fluids throughout the day to avoid dehydration.

- As the disease progresses, be aware of the increased risk of choking because of chewing and swallowing problems.
- Maintain routine dental checkups and daily oral health care to keep the mouth and teeth healthy.

ACTIVITIES

What to do all day? Finding activities that the person with AD can do and is interested in can be a challenge. Building on current skills generally works better than trying to teach something new.

- Don't expect too much. Simple activities often are best, especially when they use current abilities.
- Help the person get started on an activity. Break the activity down into small steps and praise the person for each step he or she completes.
- Watch for signs of agitation or frustration with an activity. Gently help or distract the person to something else.
- Incorporate activities the person seems to enjoy into the daily routine and try to do them at a similar time each day.
- Try to include the person with AD in the entire activity process. For instance, at mealtimes, encourage the person to help prepare the food, set the table, pull out the chairs, or put away the dishes. This can help maintain functional skills, enhance feelings of personal control, and make good use of time.
- Take advantage of adult day services, which provide various activities for the person with AD, as well as an opportunity for caregivers to gain temporary relief from tasks associated with caregiving. Transportation and meals often are provided.

EXERCISE

Incorporating exercise into the daily routine has benefits for both the person with AD and the caregiver. Not only can it improve health, but it also can provide a meaningful activity for both of you to share.

- Think about what kind of physical activities you both enjoy, perhaps walking, swimming, tennis, dancing, or gardening. Determine the time of day and place where this type of activity would work best.

- Be realistic in your expectations. Build slowly, perhaps just starting with a short walk around the yard, for example, before progressing to a walk around the block.

- Be aware of any discomfort or signs of overexertion. Talk to the person's doctor if this happens.

- Allow as much independence as possible.

- See what kinds of exercise programs are available in your area. Senior centers may have group programs for people who enjoy exercising with others. Local malls often have walking clubs and provide a place to exercise when the weather is bad.

- Encourage physical activities. Spend time outside when the weather permits. Exercise often helps everyone sleep better.

INCONTINENCE

As the disease progresses, many people with AD begin to experience incontinence, or the inability to control their bladder and/or bowels. Incontinence can be upsetting to the person and difficult for the caregiver. Sometimes incontinence is due to physical illness, so be sure to discuss it with the person's doctor.

- Have a routine for taking the person to the bathroom and stick to it as closely as possible. For example, take the person to the bathroom every 3 hours or so during the day. Don't wait for the person to ask.

- Watch for signs that the person may have to go to the bathroom, such as restlessness or pulling at clothes. Respond quickly.

- Be understanding when accidents occur. Stay calm and reassure the person if he or she is upset. Try to keep track of when accidents happen to help plan ways to avoid them.

- To help prevent nighttime accidents, limit certain types of fluids — such as those with caffeine — in the evening.

- If you are going to be out with the person, plan ahead. Know where restrooms are located, and have the person wear simple, easy-to-remove clothing. Take an extra set of clothing along in case of an accident.

SLEEP PROBLEMS

For the exhausted caregiver, sleep can't come too soon. For many people with AD, however, the approach of nighttime may be a difficult time. Many people with AD become restless, agitated, and irritable around dinnertime or late in the evening; this is referred to as sundowning or the sundown syndrome. Getting the person to go to bed and stay there may require some advance planning.

• Encourage exercise during the day and limit daytime napping; but make sure that the person gets adequate rest during the day because fatigue can increase the likelihood of late afternoon restlessness.

• Try to schedule more physically demanding activities earlier in the day. For example, bathing could be earlier in the morning, or large family meals could be at midday.

• Set a quiet, peaceful tone in the evening to encourage sleep. Keep the lights dim, eliminate loud noises; play soothing music if the person seems to enjoy it.

• Try to keep bedtime at a similar time each evening. Developing a bedtime routine may help.

• Restrict access to caffeine late in the day.

• For safety, use night-lights in the bedroom, hall, and bathroom, or if the darkness is frightening or disorienting.

HALLUCINATIONS AND DELUSIONS

As the disease progresses, a person with AD may experience hallucinations and/or delusions. Hallucinations are when the person sees, hears, smells, tastes, or feels something that is not there. Delusions are false beliefs from which the person cannot be dissuaded.

• Sometimes hallucinations and delusions are signs of physical illness. Keep track of what the person is experiencing and discuss it with the doctor.

• Avoid arguing with the person about what he or she sees or hears. Try to respond to the feelings he or she is expressing, and provide reassurance and comfort.

• Try to distract the person to another topic or activity. Sometimes moving to another room or going outside for a walk may help.

- Turn off the television set when violent or disturbing programs are on. The person with AD may not be able to distinguish television programming from reality.
- Make sure the person is safe and does not have access to anything he or she could use to harm anyone.

WANDERING

Keeping the person safe is one of the most important aspects of caregiving. Some people with AD have a tendency to wander away from their home or their caregiver. Knowing what to do to limit wandering can protect a person from getting lost.

- Make sure that the person carries some kind of identification or wears a medical bracelet. Consider enrolling the person in the Alzheimer's Association Safe Return program if the program is available in your area. If the person gets lost and is unable to communicate adequately, identification will alert others to the person's medical condition. Notify neighbors and local authorities in advance that the person has a tendency to wander.
- Keep a recent photograph or videotape of the person with AD to assist police if the person becomes lost.
- Keep doors locked. Consider a keyed deadbolt or an additional lock up high or down low on the door. If the person can open a lock because it is familiar, a new latch or lock may help.

HOME SAFETY

Caregivers of people with AD often have to look at their homes through new eyes to identify and correct safety risks. Creating a safe environment can prevent many stressful and dangerous situations.

- Be sure to secure or put away anything that could cause danger, both inside and outside the house.
- Install secure locks on all outside windows and doors, especially if the person is prone to wandering. Remove the locks on bathroom doors to prevent the person from accidentally locking himself or herself in.

- Use childproof latches on kitchen cabinets and anyplace where cleaning supplies or other chemicals are kept.
- Label medications and keep them locked up. Also make sure knives, lighters and matches, and guns are secured and out of reach.
- Keep the house free from clutter. Remove scatter rugs and anything else that might contribute to a fall. Make sure lighting is good both inside and out.
- Be alert to and address kitchen-safety issues, such as the person forgetting to turn off the stove after cooking. Consider installing an automatic shut-off switch on the stove to prevent burns or fire.

DRIVING

Making the decision that a person with AD is no longer safe to drive is difficult, and it needs to be communicated carefully and sensitively. Even though the person may be upset by the loss of independence, safety must be the priority.

- Look for clues that safe driving is no longer possible, including getting lost in familiar places, driving too fast or too slow, disregarding traffic signs, or getting angry or confused.
- Be sensitive to the person's feelings about losing the ability to drive, but be firm in your request that he or she no longer do so. Be consistent — don't allow the person to drive on "good days" but forbid it on "bad days."
- Ask the doctor to help. The person may view the doctor as an authority and be willing to stop driving. The doctor also can contact the Department of Motor Vehicles and request that the person be reevaluated.
- If necessary, take the car keys. If just having keys is important to the person, substitute a different set of keys.
- If all else fails, disable the car or move it to a location where the person cannot see it or gain access to it.

VISITING THE DOCTOR

It is important that the person with AD receive regular medical care. Advance planning can help the trip to the doctor's office go more smoothly.

- Try to schedule the appointment for the person's best time of day. Also, ask the office staff what time of day the office is least crowded.

- Let the office staff know in advance that this person is confused. If there is something they might be able to do to make the visit go more smoothly, ask.

- Don't tell the person about the appointment until the day of the visit or even shortly before it is time to go. Be positive and matter-of-fact.

- Bring along something for the person to eat and drink and any activity that he or she may enjoy.

- Have a friend or another family member go with you on the trip, so that one of you can be with the person while the other speaks with the doctor.

COPING WITH HOLIDAYS

Holidays are bittersweet for many AD caregivers. The happy memories of the past contrast with the difficulties of the present, and extra demands on time and energy can seem overwhelming. Finding a balance between rest and activity can help.

- Keep or adapt family traditions that are important to you. Include the person with AD as much as possible.

- Recognize that things will be different, and have realistic expectations about what you can do.

- Encourage friends and family to visit. Limit the number of visitors at one time, and try to schedule visits during the time of day when the person is at his or her best.

- Avoid crowds, changes in routine, and strange surroundings that may cause confusion or agitation.

- Do your best to enjoy yourself. Try to find time for the holiday things you like to do, even if it means asking a friend or family member to spend time with the person while you are out.

- At larger gatherings such as weddings or family reunions, try to have a space available where the person can rest, be alone, or spend some time with a smaller number of people, if needed. Do not isolate them!

VISITING A PERSON WITH AD

Visitors are important to people with AD. They may not always remember who the visitors are, but the human connection has value. Here are some ideas to share with someone who is planning to visit a person with AD.

- Plan the visit for the time of day when the person with AD is at his or her best. Consider bringing along an activity, such as something familiar to read or photo albums to look at, but be prepared to skip it if he or she is not receptive.
- Be calm and quiet. Avoid using a loud tone of voice or talking to the person as if he or she were a child. Respect the person's personal space and don't get too close.
- Try to establish eye contact and call the person by name to get his or her attention. Remind the person who you are if he or she doesn't seem to recognize you.
- If the person is confused, don't argue. Respond to the feelings you hear being communicated, and distract the person to a different topic if necessary.
- If the person doesn't recognize you, is unkind, or responds angrily, remember not to take it personally. He or she is reacting out of confusion.

CHOOSING A NURSING HOME

For many caregivers, there comes a point when they are no longer able to take care of their loved one at home. Choosing a residential care facility — a nursing home or an assisted living facility — is a big decision, and it can be hard to know where to start.

- It's helpful to gather information about services and options before the need actually arises. This gives you time to explore fully all the possibilities before making a decision.
- Determine what facilities are in your area. Doctors, friends and relatives, hospital social workers, and religious organizations may be able to help you identify specific facilities.
- Make a list of questions you would like to ask the staff. Think about what is important to you, such as activity programs, transportation, or special units for people with AD.

- Contact the places that interest you and make an appointment to visit. Talk to the administration, nursing staff, and residents.
- Observe the way the facility runs and how residents are treated. You may want to drop by again unannounced to see if your impressions are the same.
- Find out what kinds of programs and services are offered for people with AD and their families. Ask about staff training in dementia care, and check to see what the policy is about family participation in planning patient care.
- Check on room availability, cost and method of payment, and participation in Medicare or Medicaid. You may want to place your name on a waiting list even if you are not ready to make an immediate decision about long-term care.
- Once you have made a decision, be sure you understand the terms of the contract and financial agreement. You may want to have a lawyer review the documents with you before signing.
- Moving is a big change for both the person with AD and the caregiver. A social worker may be able to help you plan for and adjust to the move. It is important to have support during this difficult transition.

Source: NIA, NIH, ADCAR, download at http://www.nia.nih.gov/Alzheimers/Publications/caregiver guide.htms#intro

Appendix E

Glossary

This glossary was largely derived from the Administration on Aging and is available online at — http://www.aoa.gov/siteutil/glossary.asp. For a comprehensive glossary of Medicare terms, the reader is referred to— http://www.medicare.gov/Glossary/Search.asp.

Access Services— Those services and activities designed to enhance and facilitate the awareness of and participation in programs available to elders.

Activities of Daily Living (ADLs)—Activities usually performed for oneself in the course of a normal day including toileting, bathing, dressing, grooming, eating, walking, using the telephone, taking medications, and any other personal care activities.

Administration on Aging (AoA)—The official federal agency dedicated to implement programs that provide supportive home and community-based services to older persons and their caregivers.

Administrator—A person licensed to run a nursing home; one who has received training in fiscal, legal, social and medical aspects of running such an institution.

Adult Day Care— Adult Day Care Centers offer social, recreational and health-related services to individuals in a protective setting who cannot be left alone during the day because of health care and social need, confusion or disability.

Adult Family Care Home— A full-time, licensed, family-type living arrangement in which a person or persons provide room, board, and one or more personal services, as appropriate for the level of functional impairment for three or fewer non-relatives who are elders or disabled adults.

Advance Directive—A legal document in which a person specifies which life-prolonging medical measures he or she does, and does not, want to be taken if he or she becomes terminally ill or incapacitated. Also known as a living will.

Aging Network— The agencies and organizations at the local, state, and national level involved in serving and/or representing the needs of the elderly.

Ancillary Services— Those services needed by a nursing home resident, but not provided by the nursing home, such as podiatry and dental services. Ancillary services may not be included in the basic rate of the facility.

Area Agency on Aging— A quasi-governmental entity mandated by Older Americans Act, and administered by the Administration on Aging (AoA). AoA distributes funds for various aging programs through state agencies on aging with in turn fund local area agencies on aging. Area Agencies on Aging address the concerns of older Americans at the local level. They play an important role in identifying community and social service needs and assuring that social and nutritional supports are made available to older people in communities where they live. In most cases, Area Agencies on Aging do not provide direct services. Instead, they subcontract with other organizations to facilitate the provision of a full range of services for older people.

Assessment— A written evaluation of a client's needs completed by a social worker, health care provider, or other professional that is used to determine eligibility and priority for some services and to help with developing a care plan.

Assisted Living Facility— A residential setting that provides a combination of housing and personalized health care in a professionally managed group-setting designed to respond to the individual needs of persons who require assistance with activities of daily living. The facility provides care to residents who cannot live independently, but who do not require 24 hour nursing care. Terminology varies from state to state

Assistive Technology— Any service or apparatus that helps the elderly or disabled do the activities they have always done but must now do differently. These tools are also sometimes called "adaptive devices."

Beneficiary— A person who is entitled to receive the benefits or proceeds of a will, trust, insurance policy, retirement plan, annuity or other contract.

Benefit Period— The number of years an insurance policy will provide benefits. Many long-term insurance policies offer buyers a choice of between three and five years; some offer lifetime benefits.

Benefit Trigger— A condition that must exist in order for an insurance company to pay benefits under a long-term care insurance policy.

Benefits— Monetary sums paid or payable to a person insured under an insurance policy, or to someone else, such as a health care provider, to whom the insured person has assigned the benefits.

Board and Care Home— A small to medium-sized group residence that provides residents with a private or shared room, and meals. These homes offer some assistance with activities of daily living, but not skilled nursing.

Care or Case Management— Case managers work with family members and older adults to assess, arrange and evaluate supportive efforts of seniors and their families to remain independent.

Care Manager—(Also referred to as a care coordinator or case manager). A health care professional — typically a nurse or social worker — who arranges, monitors, or coordinates long-term care services. A care manager may also assess a patient's needs and develop a plan of care, subject to approval by the patient's physician.

Caregiver— A generic term referring to a person, who is either paid or volunteers, who provides assistance to an older person with the activities of daily living, health care, financial matters, guidance, companionship and social interaction. A caregiver can provide more than one aspect of care. Most often the term refers to a family member or friend who aids the older person.

Certified— A long-term care facility, home health agency, or hospice agency that meets the requirements imposed by Medicare and Medicaid is said to be certified. Being certified is not the same as being accredited. Medicare, Medicaid and some long-term care insurance policies only cover care in a certified facility or provided by a certified agency.

Certified Nursing Assistant (CNA)—CNAs are trained and qualified to help nurses by providing non-medical assistance to patients, such as help with eating, cleaning and dressing.

Chore Service— Chore service is available to persons who are physically unable to perform tasks, such as heavy cleaning, minor repair or yard work, and unable to secure assistance from family or friends nor have the means to pay privately.

Chronic Illness or Condition— An illness or other condition with one or more of the following characteristics — permanency, residual disability, requires rehabilitation training, or requires a long period of supervision, observation, or care. Typically, it is a disease or condition that lasts over a long period of time and cannot be cured; it is often associated with disability.

Chronically Ill Individual— According to federal law, a person who, within the preceding 12-month period, has been certified by a licensed health care practitioner as:

1. being unable to perform, without substantial assistance from another person, at least two activities of daily living for a period of at least ninety consecutive days due to a loss of functional capacity; or

2. requiring substantial supervision to protect such a person from threats to health and safety due to severe cognitive impairment.

Codicil — A written amendment to a will.

Cognitive Impairment — Deterioration of intellectual ability, such as disorientation as to people, places or time; impairment of short-term or long-term memory; and/or impairment of one's ability to reason; that has progressed to the extent that a person requires substantial supervision by another person. Cognitive impairment includes Alzheimer's disease and senile dementia. The existence of cognitive impairment is determined by clinical evidence and standardized tests that reliably measure the person's impairment

Coinsurance — For Medicare, it is the percentage of the Medicare-approved amount that you have to pay after you pay the deductible for Part A and/or Part B. For other types of health insurance, it is usually a percentage of billed charges after you pay the deductible.

Community-Based Services — Services designed to enable the elderly to live independently in their own homes, such as adult day care and senior centers.

Companionship Services — Companions visit isolated and homebound elders for conversation, reading, and light errands.

Congregate Meals — These programs provide older individuals with free or low cost, nutritionally sound meals served five days a week in easily accessible locations — typically senior centers, community centers, and schools. Besides promoting better health through improved nutrition, meal programs provide daily activities and socialization for participants which help reduce the isolation of old age.

Conservator — An individual who is appointed by a court to assume responsibility for a child, or for an adult who is not capable of managing his or her own affairs.

Continuing Care Retirement Community (CCRC) — A retirement community that offers a broad range of services and levels of care based on what each resident needs over time. Sometimes called "life care," this can range from independent living in an apartment to assisted living to full-time care in a nursing home. Residents move from one setting to another based on their needs. Care in CCRCs can be expensive, with a large payment often required before moving in, and monthly fees thereafter.

179

Coordination of Benefits— A provision in a health insurance plan that tells which health plan or insurance policy pays first if two health plans or insurance policies cover the same benefits. If one of the plans is Medicare, federal law may determine who pays first.

Co-payment— A charge you pay for a specific medical service.

Covered Benefit or Service— A health service or item that is included in an insurance plan or policy, and that is paid for either partially or fully.

Covered Charge— Services or benefits for which a health plan makes either partial or full payment.

Cueing—Directing or supervising the actions of someone with cognitive impairment (for example, showing them how to eat, reminding them which medications to take at the appropriate times, giving visual or verbal reminders for dressing or toileting, etc.).

Custodial Care— Personal care to help individuals meet their needs in ADLs. Someone without professional training may provide this type of care. In most cases, Medicare does not pay for custodial care.

Deductible— The amount the individual must pay, in a given year, before his or her health insurance or Medicare begins to pay benefits.

Dementia—Deterioration of intellectual abilities (e.g., vocabulary, abstract thinking, judgment, memory loss, physical coordination), the loss of which interferes with daily activities.

Depression—This is one of the most undiagnosed conditions among seniors. But, with proper medical care, depression is a reversible psychiatric condition. Symptoms include a persistent sad, anxious or "empty" mood, loss of interest or pleasure in activities once enjoyed, and difficulty sleeping.

Discharge Planner—A social worker or other health care professional who assists hospital patients and their families in transitioning from the hospital to another level of care such as rehabilitation in a skilled nursing facility, home health care in the patient's home, or long-term care in a nursing home.

Domicile— A person's permanent legal residence.

Durable Medical Equipment (DME)—Medical equipment that is ordered by a physician or other health care provider for use in the home — examples are walkers, wheelchairs, and hospital beds. DME is paid for under both Medicare Part B and Part A for home health services.

Durable Power of Attorney — Also known as a Power of Attorney for Health Care. A written legal document in which one person (the principal) appoints another person to make health care decisions on behalf of the principal in the event the principal becomes incapacitated (the document defines incapacitation). This instrument can contain instructions about specific medical treatment that should be applied or withheld.

Elder Abuse — Elder abuse is a term referring to any knowing, intentional, or negligent act by a caregiver or any other person that causes harm or a serious risk of harm to a vulnerable adult. The specificity of laws varies from state to state, but broadly defined, abuse may be physical, emotional, sexual, exploitation, neglect, and abandonment.

Elder Abuse Prevention Programs — Allegations of abuse, neglect and exploitation of senior citizens are investigated by highly trained protective service specialists. Intervention is provided in instances of substantiated elder abuse, neglect or exploitation.

Elder Care — A wide range of services provided at home, in the community and in residential care facilities, including assisted living facilities and nursing homes. It includes health-related services such as rehabilitative therapies, skilled nursing, and palliative care, as well as supervision and a wide range of supportive personal care and social services.

Eldercare Locator — Developed by the U.S. Administration on Aging, the Eldercare Locator is a free nationwide directory assistance service. It helps older people and their caregivers find local support services to help them live independently in their own community. Eldercare Locator can be found at — http://www.elder care.gov/Eldercare/Public/Home.asp.

Energy Assistance — These programs can provide low-income elderly homeowners and renters with funds to help pay home utility and heating costs. Eligibility requirements may vary from state to state.

Estate — The totality of a decedent's assets and debts at the time of his or her death.

Estate Tax — A tax levied on a person's estate after that person's death.

Exclusion — A health condition, situation, item, service or expense that an insurance policy does not cover. Medicare excludes coverage for most prescription drugs, long-term care, and custodial care in a nursing or private home.

Executor — The person or institution appointed in a will, or by a court, to settle the estate of a deceased person.

Friendly Visitors and Telephone Reassurance —These programs, which have different titles in different communities, provide regular personal or telephone contact for older persons who are homebound or live alone. Usually a volunteer provides the service. Besides developing friendships, perhaps a more important aspect of these programs is the volunteer's ability to identify needs of the individual as they occur and notify those who can help.

Geriatric Care Managers — Individuals specifically trained in geriatric care management, who provide case management services on a fee-for-service basis to individual clients.

Geriatrician —A physician who specializes in the care of the elderly, primarily those who are frail and have complex medical and social problems.

Grantor —The person who creates a trust.

Guardian —An individual appointed by a court of law to manage a person's financial and/or personal affairs because the court has found that the person is not competent to manage his or her own affairs. A conservator is similarly appointed, but only for financial affairs.

Guardianship —The process in which an individual is appointed by a court of law to manage a person's financial and/or personal affairs because the person is not able to or is not competent to manage his/her own affairs

Home and Community-Based Services —A variety of supportive services delivered in community settings or in an older person's home are designed to help older persons remain living at home and avoid institutionalization.

Home Delivered Meals —Sometimes referred to as "meals on wheels," home delivered meals delivered to homebound persons who are unable to prepare their own meals and have no outside assistance.

Home Health Care —A variety of health services that are provided in a home health care program in the patient's home, under the direction of a physician.

Home Modification —Adaptation and/or renovation to the living environment intended to increase ease of use, safety, security and independence.

Homemaker Service —Homemaker service is extended to individuals who are unable to perform day-to-day household duties and have no one available to assist them.

Hospice — Usually a combination of at-home and hospital care of the terminally ill that combines medical and social services. Hospice care involves a team-oriented approach that addresses the medical, physical, social, emotional and spiritual needs of the patient, the family, and caregivers. This approach emphasizes pain control, symptom management, and emotional support rather than life-sustaining equipment. Hospice services are covered under Medicare Part A.

Incontinence—The inability to control urination, bowel movements or both.

Information and Referral—Information Specialists are available to provide assistance and linkage to available services and resources.

Inheritance Tax—A tax that is levied by a state or local government upon those who inherit property; paid by the recipient.

Inpatient Care—Health care that receive when you are admitted to a hospital or skilled nursing facility.

Instrumental Activities of Daily Living (IADLs)—These are tasks that, in addition to activities of daily living, an individual must be able to perform in order to live independently (without the assistance or substantial supervision of another person). Examples include grocery shopping, meal preparation, using the telephone, laundry, light housekeeping, bill paying, and managing your medications.

Inter Vivos Trust—A revocable trust created during someone's lifetime to hold assets during that person's lifetime, thereby removing those assets from probate at death; also called a living trust.

Intestate—Dying without a legal will.

Irrevocable Trust—A trust that, once executed, cannot be revoked or changed without the consent of the beneficiary.

Joint Tenancy in Common—A type of joint tenancy of property without right of survivorship. Upon the death of any joint tenant, his or her ownership interest is transferred according to the terms of his or her will that may, or may not, provide for transfer to a surviving joint tenant(s).

Joint Tenancy with Right of Survivorship—A type of ownership of property by two or more persons in which each owns an interest in the whole. Upon the death of any joint tenant, his or her ownership interest automatically passes to the surviving joint tenant(s).

Lapse—Termination of a policy when a required premium has not been paid by the end of the policy's specified grace period.

Legal Assistance—Legal advice and representation is available to persons aged 60 and over for certain types of legal matters including government program benefits, tenant rights, and consumer problems.

Life Tenancy —Under this arrangement, an owner sells a home, and he or she then leases it back and receives a written guarantee that he or she can continue to live in the home for the rest of his or her life.

Living Trust —A trust created during someone's lifetime to hold assets during that person's lifetime, thereby removing those assets from probate at death. A living trust can be either revocable or irrevocable. It avoids probate and therefore gets assets distributed significantly faster than a will.

Living Will —A legal document in which a person specifies which life-prolonging medical measures he or she does, and does not, want to be taken if he or she becomes terminally ill or incapacitated. Also known as an advance directive.

Long Term Care —A general term that describes a range of medical, nursing, custodial, social, and community services designed to help people with chronic health impairments or forms of dementia. Long-term care can be provided at home, in the community, or in various types of facilities, including nursing homes and assisted living facilities. Most long-term care is custodial care. Medicare does not pay for this type of care if this is the only kind of care the individual requires.

Long Term Care Insurance —This type of insurance policy is designed to cover long term care expenses in a facility or at home.

Long Term Care Ombudsman —Long term care ombudsmen, state and local, work cooperatively with nursing homes and board and care facilities to improve the quality of life for residents. They serve as patient's rights advocates, investigating and negotiating resolutions to concerns voiced by residents in matters of resident services and care.

Medicaid —A joint Federal and State program that helps with medical costs for some people with low incomes and limited resources and who meet other eligibility requirements. Medicaid programs vary from state to state, but most health care costs are covered if you qualify for both Medicare and Medicaid. Medicaid may also pay for nursing home care if the individual's income and assets are within certain limits.

Medically Necessary —Services or supplies that are needed for the diagnosis or treatment of your medical condition, meet the standards of good medical practice in the local area, and are not mainly for the convenience of you or your doctor.

Medicare —The national health insurance program for eligible people 65 and older and some disabled individuals. Part A covers hospital costs. Part B covers doctor bills and other medical costs.

Medicare Supplement Insurance —A private insurance policy that covers many of the gaps in Medicare coverage (also known as Medigap Insurance or Medicare Supplemental Insurance).

Medigap —Medigap is designed specifically to supplement and complement Medicare's benefits by filling in some of the gaps of Medicare coverage. Medigap insurance policies are non-group policies that may pay for Medicare deductibles, prescription drugs, or other services not covered by Medicare.

Non-formulary drugs —Drugs not on a plan's approved drug list.

Nursing Home —A state-licensed residential facility that provides a room, meals, help with activities of daily living, recreation, and general nursing care to people who are chronically ill or unable to take care of their daily living needs. It may also be called a Long Term Care Facility. If it has been certified as such by Medicare, it is also referred to as a Skilled Nursing Facility.

Occupational Therapist —A rehabilitation professional who teaches individuals to compensate for functional limitations as a result of an injury, illness or disability by learning skills and techniques needed to perform activities of daily living and optimize independence.

PACE (Programs of All-inclusive Care for the Elderly)—PACE combines medical, social, and long-term care services for frail people to help people stay independent and living in their community as long as possible, while getting the high-quality care they need. PACE is available only in states that have chosen to offer it under Medicaid.

Para-transit Services —Specialized transportation, such as a wheelchair accessible van, for seniors and other people with disabilities. These services may offer transportation to senior centers, medical care, shopping malls, or specific appointments.

Personal Emergency Response System —In case of a fall or other medical emergency, this electronic device enables the user to contact help 24-hours-a-day simply by pressing a button.

Physical Therapist —A rehabilitation professional who utilizes various therapies to help people maximize mobility, and restore strength and body movement after an illness or injury such as a stroke, fall, back injury, etc.

Plan of Care —The written plan that describes the services and care that are most appropriate and therapeutic for an individual patient.

Power of Attorney —A written legal document in which one person (the principal) appoints another person to manage the principal's financial affairs.

Power of Attorney for Health Care — Also known as a Durable Power of Attorney. A written legal document in which one person (the principal) appoints another person to make health care decisions on behalf of the principal in the event the principal becomes incapacitated (the document defines incapacitation). This instrument can contain instructions about specific medical treatment that should be applied or withheld.

Pre-existing Condition — An illness or disability for which a person was treated or advised within a certain time period (typically 6–12 months) before applying for an insurance policy. Any pre-existing condition would typically not be covered during a designated time period after the effective date of the policy.

Preferred Provider Organization (PPO) — Another type of managed care plan. Members have a choice of utilizing healthcare providers in the PPO network, or hospitals, doctors and other healthcare professionals outside the plan for an additional cost.

Primary Care Physician — A doctor who is trained to give you basic care. Your primary care doctor is the doctor you see first for most health problems. He or she makes sure that you get the care that you need to keep you healthy. He or she may consult with other physicians and health care providers about your care and refer you to them. In many HMOs, you must see your primary care doctor before you can see any other health care provider.

Primary Caregiver — The person, usually the spouse or adult child, who takes on the primary day-to-day responsibility of caring for the physical, psychological and social needs of another person.

Probate — The process by which an executor (if there is a will), or a court-appointed administrator (if there is no will), manages and distributes a decedent's property to heirs or beneficiaries.

Provider — A properly-licensed doctor, health care professional, hospital, or other health care facility, including a home health agency, that provides health care or related social services.

Rehabilitation — Those services that are ordered by your doctor to help you recover from an illness or injury. These may be provided by nurses, and/or physical, occupational, and speech therapists.

Respite Care — The provision of short-term relief (respite) to families or other individuals caring for frail elders offers tremendous potential for maintaining dependent persons in the least restrictive environment. Respite services encompass traditional home-based care, as well as adult day health, skilled nursing, home health aide and short term institutional care. Respite can vary in time from part of a day to several weeks.

Senior Centers —A vital link in the service delivery network which older persons may avail themselves of, senior centers are functioning as meal sites, screening clinics, recreational centers, social service agency branch offices, mental health counseling clinics, older worker employment agencies, volunteer coordinating centers, and community meeting halls.

Skilled Care —A type of health care given when you need skilled nursing or rehabilitation staff to manage, observe, and evaluate your care.

State Agency on Aging —The Older Americans Act mandates that each state have a state agency on aging which is part of state government. The State Agency on Aging is the designated focal point within the state government responsible for administering a complex service system designed to complement and support other human service systems in meeting the needs of the elderly.

State Health Insurance Information Counseling and Assistance Programs — Known as SHIP, this program is comprised of 53 state programs and nearly 15,000 trained volunteers who offer unbiased, one on one counseling to assist Medicare beneficiaries understand their health insurance benefits and options.

Subsidized Senior Housing— A type of program, available through the Federal Department of Housing and Urban Development (HUD) and some States, to help people with low or moderate incomes pay for housing.

Telemedicine/Telenursing —Professional services given to a patient through an interactive telecommunications system by a practitioner at a distant site.

Transportation —Programs that provide door-to-door transportation for people who may be elderly or disabled, who do not have private transportation and who are unable to utilize public transportation to meet their needs.

Selected Readings

In addition to this selected list of publications, the reader will find Appendices A, B, C, and D very useful. Many of the websites listed in the Online Resources chapter also include links to publications on every conceivable topic of interest to caregivers.

––––––––––––––––––––

AARP. "Valuing the Invaluable: The Economic Value of Family Caregiving." http://www.aarp.org/research/housing-mobility/caregiving/i13_caregiving.html, December 29, 2008.

AARP. National Alliance for Caregiving. *Caregiving in the U.S. 2009*. http://www.aarp.org/research/surveys/care/ltc/hc/articles/caregiving_09.html, November 2009.

_____. _____. *A Focused Look at Those Caring for Someone Age 50 or Older*. http://assets.aarp.org/rgcenter/il/caregiving_09_es50.pdf, November 2009.

American Geriatric Society, Foundation for Health in Aging. *Eldercare at Home—A Comprehensive Online Guide for Family Caregivers*. http://www.healthinaging.org/public_education/eldercare/1.xml, No date.

AXA Equitable Life Insurance Company. *Aging Parents and Common Sense: A Directory of Resources for You and Your Parents*. http://www.caregiving.org/pubs/brochures/Aging%20Parent-Directory_5thEd.pdf, April 2006.

_____. *Aging Parents and Common Sense: A Practical Guide for You and Your Parents*. http://www.caregiving.org/pubs/brochures/Aging%20Parent-Guide_5thEd.pdf, April 2006.

Centers for Medicare and Medicaid. *Guide to Choosing a Nursing Home*. http://www.medicare.gov/Publications/Pubs/pdf/02174.pdf, November 2008.

Coon, David W. *Lesbian, Gay, Bisexual and Transgender (LGBT) Issues and Family Caregiving*. http://www.caregiver.org/caregiver/jsp/content/pdfs/op_2003_lgbt_issues.pdf, August 2003.

Corcoran, Mary A. *Practical Skills Training for Family Caregivers*. http://www.caregiver.org/caregiver/jsp/content/pdfs/op_2003_skills_training.pdf, August 2003.

Hunt, Gail. "Nearly a Third of All US Adults Are Now Family Caregivers—65.7 Million." http://caregivershome.com/news/article.cfm?UID=2341, December 15, 2009.

Johnson, Richard W., and Joshua M. Wiener. *A Profile of Frail Older Americans and Their Caregivers.* http://www.urban.org/publications/311284.html, March 1, 2006.

MetLife. January 2007. *Resources for Caregivers.* http://www.caregiving.org/pubs/bro chures/resourcesforcaregivers07.pdf.

National Alliance for Caregiving. *Care for the Family Caregiver: A Place to Start.* http:// www.caregiving.org/pubs/brochures/CFC.pdf, December 2005.

National Institute on Aging. *Talking with Your Doctor.* http://www.niapublications. org/pubs/talking/index.asp, April 2008.

Pew Research Center. "Baby Boomers: From the Age of Aquarius to the Age of Responsibility." http://pewsocialtrends.org/pubs/306/baby-boomers-from-the-age-of-aquarius-to-the-age-of-responsibility, December 8, 2005.

_____. *Growing Old in America: Expectation vs. Reality.* http://pewsocialtrends.org/assets/pdf/Getting-Old-in-America.pdf, June 22, 2009.

Rosenblatt, Bob, and Carol Van Steenberg. *Handbook for Long-Distance Caregivers.* http://www.caregiver.org/caregiver/jsp/content_node.jsp?nodeid=1034, 2003.

U.S. Federal Trade Commission. *Funerals: A Consumer Guide.* http://www.ftc.gov/bcp/edu/pubs/consumer/products/pro19.pdf, No date.

Index